Wilsons'

Coca-Cola

TRADE MARK
R.E.G. U.S. PAT. OFF.

Price Guide

Revised
3rd Edition

Helen & Al
Wilson

Schiffer Publishing Ltd

4880 Lower Valley Road, Atglen, PA 19310 USA

ACKNOWLEDGMENTS

Julie and Bob Carter
Bert Hansen
Fred Mosrie
Belle Poppenheimer
Ann and Dave Sherrod
Neil Wood
Sam's Town Casino

Revised price guide: 2000
Copyright © 1994, 1997 & 2000 by Al and Helen Wilson
Library of Congress Catalog Card Number: 99-68546

ISBN: 0-7643-0983-8
Printed in China
1 2 3 4

Published by Schiffer Publishing Ltd.
4880 Lower Valley Road
Atglen, PA 19310
Phone: (610) 593-1777; Fax: (610) 593-2002
E-mail: Schifferbk@aol.com
Please visit our web site catalog at **www.schifferbooks.com**

In Europe, Schiffer books are distributed by Bushwood Books
6 Marksbury Avenue Kew Gardens
Surrey TW9 4JF England
Phone: 44 (0)208-392-8585; Fax: 44 (0)208-392-9876
E-mail: Bushwd@aol.com

This book may be purchased from the publisher.
Include $3.95 for shipping. Please try your bookstore first.
We are interested in hearing from authors with book ideas on related subjects.
You may write for a free printed catalog.

CONTENTS

SLOGANS

1886— "Coca-Cola—Delicious, Refreshing, Exhilarating"

1905— "Coca-Cola Revives and Sustains"

1906— "Great National Temperance Beverage"

1917— "Three Million a Day"

1922— "Thirst Knows No Season"

1929— "The Pause That Refreshes"

1932— "Ice Cold Sunshine"

1938— "The Best Friend Thirst Ever Had"

1948— "Where There's A Coke, There's Hospitality"

1949— "Coca-Cola— Along the Highway to Anywhere"

1957— "Sign of Good Taste"

1963— "Things Go Better With Coke"

1970— "It's the Real Thing"

1971— "I'd Like To Buy The World A Coke"

1976— "Coke Adds Life"

1979— "Have a Coke and a Smile"

1982— "Coke Is It"

1986— "Catch the Wave—Red, White and You"

1992— "You Can't Beat the Real Thing"

Almost 60 million servings to more than 40 million people everyday in America.

GRADING

Grading pieces for purchase (especially over the telephone) can be confusing. Here are the standard terms:

MINT: New condition, in original wrapper or box, no marks or scratches visible.

NEAR MINT: Might appear to be Mint, but close inspection shows minor marks, a slight tear, small crazing, etc...usually sold for Mint.

EXCELLENT: Only minor hairline scratches, small chips or marks on the edges...NO RUST on front part of item.

VERY GOOD: About the same as Excellent, except minor flaking and fading, pinhead rust spot, small dent or tear, but not on main part of the picture.

GOOD: Small dents, scratches, pitting, fading, rust; crazing could be used as a filler.

POOR: All of the above-mentioned faults. A rare piece in poor condition might tempt a collector, but its value is NIL.

We receive phone calls from people with Coke items for sale. They ask high prices for merchandise they refer to as "really good, almost mint, hardly any dents, just a little rust.." etcetera. PEOPLE DO NOT KNOW HOW TO GRADE. The six categories outlined above can be confusing. We find that "over the phone" buying is safer and more realistic if a scale of 1-10 is used.

PREFACE

Only in modern times have people's artifacts been collected, categorized and codified almost immediately after their production...like Coca-Cola memorabilia has been. We live in a century when last year's styles are out of date — referred to as "has beens." In the midst of our fickle folly, Coca-Cola has kept careful track of each season's yearly whims. They flowed with Art Nouveau and Art Deco influence...the Roaring '20s...'30s Depression...Wartime...Pop-Art '60s...TV innovations...Hollywood stars...along with the timeless Americana of artists like Elvgren, Andrew Wyeth and Norman Rockwell. Through the years, Coca-Cola has remained faithful to its tried-and-true red and white banners, and to its theme of providing "the PAUSE that REFRESHES"!

About twenty years ago a rumble began in Atlanta. Like Paul Revere, people were going from town to town - passing the word about the hunt for Coca-Cola memorabilia. This led to much publicity for the producers and the seekers. Today, 7500 members of The Coca-Cola Collectors Club keep the fires of envy burning. Also, 25 foreign countries now have 250 members who frequent the States to try their luck.

To all our friends...We know you will enjoy our new, all-color price guide. We are very excited about the several thousand items pictured, some of which have never been shown in any book before. The values given for these pieces are reasonable estimates of current market prices for MINT or NEAR MINT pieces. They were gleaned from our extensive travels throughout the country—auctions, antique markets and personal sales and collections—and some of the pricing reflects regional differences. While we can provide a general guide, individual collectors must be responsible for making their own decisions.

"Man is the only animal who drinks when he isn't thirsty."
—Mark Twain

TRAYS

*Trays that have been reproduced or made into fantasy

All trays are 10-1/2" x 13-1/4

1910. $1300*.

1913. $1100*.

1914. $750*.

1920. $900.

1921. $900.

1922. $900.

1923. $500.

1924, maroon (shown) or brown border. $900. $750.

1925. $450.

1926. $800.

1927. $750.

1928. $700.

1928. $700.

1929, glass. $450.

1929, bottle. $550.

1930. $400.

1930. $400.

1931, Rockwell. $950.

1932. $750.

1933. $500.

1934. $1000.

1935, Madge Evans. $450.

1936. $450.

1937. $425*.

1938. $325.

1939. $325.

1940. $325.

1941. $325.

1942. $400.

1950s, screened back-ground. $125.

1950s, solid back-ground. $150.

7

1950s, French. $100.

1953, English. $110.

1953, French. $110.

1950s, Spanish. $110.

1957, French rooster. $125.

1957, English rooster. $150.

1957, English umbrella girl. $350.

1957, French umbrella girl. $300.

1976, limited edition by Fred Harvey. $30.

1980, McDonald's 25th Anniversary. $60.

1976, 21st Olympiad, Montreal. $150.

1982, Pembroke Plant, Miami, FLA. $175.

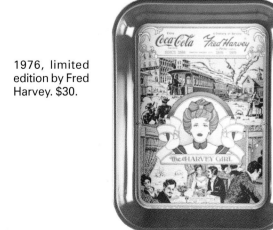

1980s, Coke collage. $20.

1981, Kansas City National Convention. $50.

1957, Hilda Clark. $25.

1957, English bird house. $225.

1957, French bird house. $200.

1957, English. $150.

1957, French. $125.

1961, "Pansy Garden". $60.

1958, English and French. $75 ea.

1961, "Pansy Garden". $60.

1961, "Pansy Garden". Rare. $85.

1968, Canadian commemorative tray in English. $85.

1968, Canadian commemorative tray in French. $60.

1969, Canadian tray in English. $90.

1969, French. $65.

1979, "Romance," and 1977, "Wedding." $200 pr.

The art work was copyrighted by the Coca-Cola Company, Atlanta, Georgia, and approved 1916. This was part of the European Zone Plantation Life Series. 5000 pairs only. Limited edition - inspired by the classic "Roots."

MEXICAN TRAYS

1940s. $550.

1960s. $100.

1960s. $85.

1962. $35.

1960s. $30.

1969. $65.

1970. $30.

1970. $35.

1965. $85.

1970. $25.

CHANGE OR TIP TRAYS

Oval trays are 4-1/4" x 6".

1900, 6". $3200.

1901, 6". $2800.

1903, 6". $2600.

1903, 4". $1900.

1906, 4". $1200.

1907. $900.

1909. $650.

1910. $650.

1913. $650.

914. $500.

1916. $400.

1920. $500.

SERVING TRAYS

1903, "Hilda Clark," 15" x 18-1/2". $5500.

1916, "Elaine," 18-1/2" x 19". $700.

1909, "St. Louis Fair," 13-1/2 x 16-1/2". $2800.

1920, "Garden Girl," 13-1/4 x 16-1/2". $1000.

1914, "Betty," 12-1/2" x 15-1/4". $950.

1913, Hamilton King, artist. 12-1/4" x 15-1/4". $1200.

1905, Lillian Nordica with bottle, 10-1/2" x 13". $3900.

1907, "Relieves Fatigue," 13-1/4" x 10-1/2". $3600.

1900, 9-1/4". $8000.

1906, "Juanita", 10-1/2" x 13-1/4". $3000.

1903, "Hilda Clark," 9-1/4". $7200.

1903, "Hilda Clark," 9-3/4". $7000.

1901, A particularly rare "Hilda Clark," 9-1/4". $5000.

TOPLESS TRAYS & VIENNA ART PLATES

1908, The Coca-Cola "topless tray." $6000.

Vienna art plate, complete with frame and black shadow box. $1000.

Vienna art plate, with frame and black shadow box. $1000.

1903, Bottle tray, 5-1/2". $5200. (not shown: bottle tray, 9-3/4". $6700.)

One of many "exquisite frames used on the plates." $500.

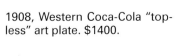

Vienna art plate only. $550.

1908, Western Coca-Cola "topless" art plate. $1400.

MENU BOARDS

1930s, tin, chalk type, 19" x 27". $275.

1930s, "Kay Display," wood with metal trim, 14" x 36". $350.

1930s, "Kay Display," wood silhouette, 14" x 24". $475.

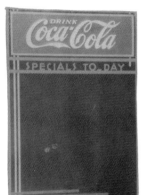

1930s, tin, chalk type, 19" x 27". $225.

1950s, porcelain, black Canada. $200.

FRIED CHICKEN	25
CHERRY PIE	10
CHICKEN SOUP	5
COCOANUT CUSTARD PIE	15
FRANKFURTER ON ROLL	10
APPLE PIE	20
GRIDDLE CAKES & SYRUP	10
ITALIAN SPAGHETTI	15
LIVERWURST SANDWICH	10
SIRLOIN STEAK	30
TEA OR COFFEE	5

1960s, reverse on glass with a metal frame, 18" x 36". $350.

1940s, reverse on glass, with metal frame, 14" x 22". $300.

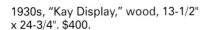

1960s, reverse on glass with a metal frame, 18" x 36". $350.

1930s, "Kay Display," wood, 13-1/2" x 24-3/4". $400.

1930s, wooden double board with metal bottle ornaments, 12" x 36". $500.

14

1903, soda menu on back, 4" x 6". $800

1940s, Kresges, 5-1/4" x 6-3/4". $5

1940s, Kresges, 5-1/4" x 6-3/4". $5

1940s, 5-3/4" x 8". $5

1950s, from Kresges, 7" x 10-1/2". $5

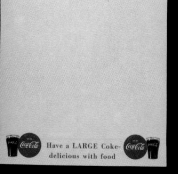

1950s, 5-3/4" x 8-1/2". $5

1950s, fillers for menu holders. $3 ea.

1960s, 7" x 10". $7

1960s, 14" x 10". $10

1897, "Victorian Girl" hanging trade card, cardboard, 6-1/2" x 10-1/2", extremely rare. $9000.

This menu cover (from The Bottling Plant in Boulder City, Nevada) was copied from the original Victorian Girl card. That valuable card belonged to the owner of The Bottling Plant when he opened the restaurant. There are only a few replicas of this menu still in existence.

The original "Victorian Girl" trade card is on display at the Calamity Jane Ice Cream Parlour in Sam's Town Casino, Las Vegas, Nevada.

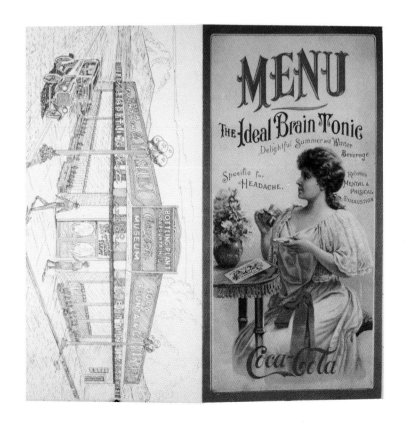

LARGE GLOSS DIVIDERS - WINDOW DISPLAYS

1931, large bottle display with circle. $500.

BOTTLES

1920s, leaded glass display. $10,000.

1920s, lamp with embossed base, 20". $6500.

1930s, 20" glass display with cap,
Dec. 25, 1923. $425.

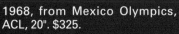

1968, from Mexico Olympics,
ACL, 20". $325.

1930s, glass, with cap, D-105529, 20".
$475.

1968, with cap, ACL, 20".
$250.

1976, with cap, ACL, 20".
$200.

1960s, plastic, with cap, 20".
$125.

1930s, white chalk, D-105529, 20",
rare. $600.

1977, with cap, ACL, 20".
$200.

1971, root commemorative bottle with box & presentation tag - complete, rare. $550.

30 oz., script - Rochester, N.Y. $225.

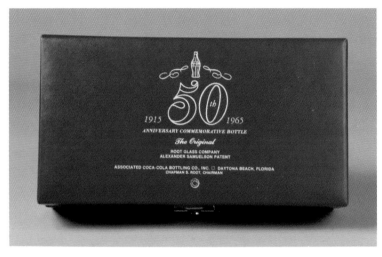

1971, front of box for commemorative root bottle.

Capped water bottle, green glass, with embossed horse. $175.

Capped water bottle, green glass, with embossed sailing ship. $150.

Logo on embossed horse and ship bottles.

Verner Springs bottle, aqua
glass, Greenville, S.C. $75.

1920s, premix bottle
in sleeve. $50.

Gold-coated, produced in
many cities, 6-1/2". $30.

C. 1915, clear bottle, from Caddo
Bottling Co., very rare. $200.

Nov. 1915, aqua. Cincinnati,
Ohio. $50.

C. 1915, clear bottle, from Denver, CO. $90.

1936, aqua. Best by Dam
Site, Las Vegas, NV. $200.

1910, aqua. By M.F. Mauer,
Muncie, IN. $125.

Dec. 25, 1923, aqua. Christmas bottle, Muncie, Indiana. $40.

1937, aqua glass, Cincinnati, Ohio, D-105529. $35.

1922, soda water bottle, William Penn embossed face, Richmond, IN. $20.

1922, aqua glass, William Penn embossed face, Richmond, IN. $20.

Amber, circle and arrow, Louisville, KY. $125.

Amber, straight arrow, Cincinnati, OH. $150.

1917, amber senate bottle, Dayton, OH. $200.

Amber, straight arrow, Cincinnati, OH. $150.

1910, amber Fosler BTGL, Richmond, IN. $150.

1950s, plastic, 6". $35.

1987, convention bottle featuring Pete Rose, Cincinnati, OH. $125.

1987, obverse of Pete Rose bottle.

1987, Pete Rose gold signature, limited quantity. $250.

Plastic bottle caps. $5 each.

(right) 1915-1917, original paper label for 6-1/2 oz. bottle. $65.
(left) 1917-1919, original paper label for 6 oz.

Bottles encased in lucite: 8-3/4", $85; 4", $35; 10-1/2", $100.

HUTCHINSON BOTTLES

1894, first bottle ever used for Coca-Cola, Beidenharn Candy Co., Vicksburg, MS. $250.

1899, Coco-Cola bottle, Chattanooga. $700.

1899, Coca-Cola bottle, Chattanooga, rare. $1000.

(left) c. 1899, marked "Property of Coca-Cola Bottling Company." $1000.
(right) c. 1902, script letters, "Birmingham, Ala." $1000.

C. 1903, block letters, "Gadsden, Ala." $1200.

C. 1903, tallest Hutchinson bottle, Brunswick, GA. $1200.

There are only 14 different Hutchinson bottles to collect!

CHRONOLOGY OF THE GLASS PACKAGE FOR COCA-COLA

1894 ———————— 1970

Archives
The Coca-Cola Company
Atlanta, Georgia

1894 ——— 1899   1900 ——— 1916   1915   1923   1937   1957   1961   1970

Nov. 16

Dec. 25

Aug. 3
(D-105529)

Applied Color
Label (ACL)

One-Way Bottle
(OWB)

One-Way Bottle
(Plastic)

SELTZER BOTTLES & SYRUP BOTTLES

Amber, Painsville, OH. $650.

Blue, Bradford, PA. $400.

Amber, Lafayette, IN. $600.

Clear, Denver, CO, 8-1/2". $350.

Green, Winona, MN. $500.

Clear, Denver, CO, 7-1/4". $450.

Clear, Royal Palm, Terre Haute, IN. $200.

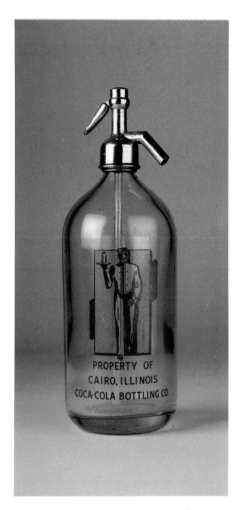

Clear, black waiter illustration, Cairo, IL. $250.

Clear, "Big Chief" illustration, Sacramento, CA. $250.

1910, syrup bottle, acid-etched wreath, metal top. $750.

1920s, syrup bottle, ACL. $700.

1920's, syrup bottle, foil label. $800.

BOTTLE RING HOLDERS

$3

$3

$8

$2

$3

$3

$15

$5

$15

$15

CARTONS & CARRIERS

1950s, aluminum, one of several styles, six-pack. $95.

1940s, Masonite with leather handle. $70.

1940s, Masonite with rope handle. $70.

1940s, bent wood with rounded corners. $150.

1950s, cardboard six-pack with Christmas sleeve. $100.

1940s, red metal, rare. $165.

1940s, bent wood, square corners. $125.

1930s, Santa cardboard, rare. $600.

1950s, metal, rare. $175.

1940s, yellow Bakelite, rare. $275.

1950s, aluminum, 12-pack. $150.

1940s, wooden, sectioned, rare. $200.

1920s, wooden with dove tail joints, rare. $250.

1940s, red and yellow painted wood with wings on each end. $175.

1950s, cardboard with metal handles. $150.

1950s, cardboard, single-bottle, for auto. $30.

1940s, cardboard, holds 24 bottles. $60.

1950s, wooden, holds 24 bottles. $60.

1950s, vinyl, holds 12 bottles. $50.

1950s, small-size picnic cooler. $250.

1940s, airline cooler, stainless liner. $375.

1950s, metal six-pack. $80.

(left) 1950s, six-pack carrier. $85.
(right) 1950s, six-pack carrier. $85.

1950s, metal stadium carrier. $175.

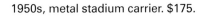

1950s, six-pack display rack. $450.

1930s, six-pack display rack. $475.

1950s, metal stadium carrier. $175.

GLASSES, PAPER CUPS, ARROW GLASS & TIN CUPS

(left) 1920, modified flare glass, 3-3/4".
$200.
(right) 1935, bell-shaped glass, 3-7/8". $65.

Bevete, multi-color. $35.

1977, cardboard cooler with flared glass. $125.

970s, 3 different sizes paper cup. $4 ea.

1940s, paper cup. $10.

1960s, 4 different sizes paper cup. $5 ea.

C. 1912, large 5-cent flare with arrow. $650.

950s, wooden cup holder. $100.

1930s, inside bottom of tin cup, Green Castle, IN, rare. $165.

DRY SERVERS & NO-DRIP BOTTLE PROTECTORS

Bottles of Coca Cola came cold, and *dripping wet*. To keep customers' hands dry, "dry servers" were invented. Most of them were 3-7/8" x 6-3/4", the perfect size to "bag" a bottle. Electric coolers made dry servers obsolete, but they are still fun to collect. Often a boxful will show up at a flea market or a Coke gathering.

1929, "The pause that refreshes." $20.

1930, "In Bottles." $15.

1934, "Good Things To Eat." $15.

1936, "Good Things To Eat." $15.

1936, "The Pause That Refreshes." $20.

1936, "And Now..." $15.

1938, "So refreshing with food." $20.

1942, "So easy to serve at home." $20.

1946, "Take a minute to refresh." $10.

1946, "Take a minute to refresh." $10.

1946, "A great drink with lunch." $10.

1946, "It's the real thing." $10.

1948, "Take off refreshed." $10.

1948, "It's the real thing." $10.

1948, "First call for refreshment." $10.

1948, "Stand by for refreshment." $10.

1948, "You can trust its quality." $10.

1948, "Refreshment right out of the bottle." $10.

1948, "Every bottle refreshes." $10.

Dry server holder which mounts on the machine. $100.

STRAWS

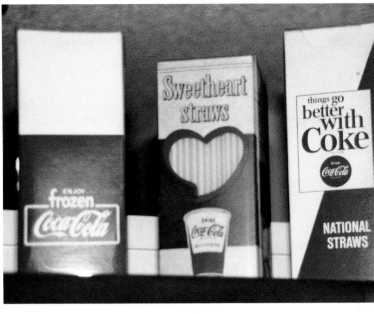

(left) 1930s, bottle straws. $100.
(center) 1930s, bottle straws. $80.
(right) 1930s, cup straws. $75.

(left) 1970s. $60.
(center) 1940s. $75.
(right) 1960s. $70.

POPCORN

1950s, cardboard megaphone popcorn holder. $60.

1950s, popcorn boxes. (left) $40. and (right) $35.

SYRUP CANS, BOTTLES & KEGS

C. 1915, both with paper labels. $300 ea.

1950s, paper label. $60.

Paper label. $30.

1900, 1 gallon jug, embossed lettering, two loops at top, rare. $600.

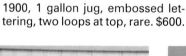

1950s, syrup can. $275.

1950s, syrup can with paper label. $275.

1960s, cover for three-page sales promotion. $45.

1960s, four-page brochure. $15.

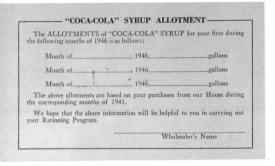

"COCA-COLA" SYRUP ALLOTMENT

The ALLOTMENTS of "COCA-COLA" SYRUP for your firm during the following months of 1946 is as follows:

Month of _____, 1946, _____ gallons

Month of _____, 1946, _____ gallons

Month of _____, 1946, _____ gallons

The above allotments are based on your purchases from our House during the corresponding months of 1941.

We hope that the above information will be helpful to you in carrying out your Rationing Program.

Wholesaler's Name

1946, syrup allotment card. $20.

1915-1922, five-gallon wooden keg with label. $275. By same manufacturer, ten-gallon keg, $300; and 55-gallon, $350. Leaded glass shade was given with purchase of 55-gallon of syrup.

1931, cardboard display, girl with tray. $500.

CALENDARS

1901, 7-3/8" x 13". $8500. (Note: This calendar shows the last page, including all of the months.) RARE.

1904, calendar featuring Lillian Nordica, the famous opera star. This calendar survived fire and water, and is so rare that it is still considered a prize. 7-3/4" x 15-1/4". $6000.

1919, small calendar featuring movie star Marion Davies, 6-1/4" x 10-1/2". Though not rare, valuable or particularly sought-after, the actress' beguiling smile and the frame's convenient size make it popular among collectors. $4500.

1912, large mint version of a Hamilton King design, 12-1/4" x 30-3/4". $7500. A smaller version, 9-3/4" x 19-3/4". $6500.

1918, June Caprice is the "other" small calendar, 5" x 9". In mint condition and properly framed. $550.

1914. $2500.

1915. $5500.

1916. $3300.

1917, Constance, with glass and bottle. $3800.

1919. $5000.

1920, with bottle. $3800.

1921. $2500.

1922. $2800.

1925. $1800.

1926. $2500.

1924. $1800.

1923, with bottle. $1400.

1927. $1500.

1928. $1500.

1929. $1800.

1930. $1800.

1931, Norman Rockwell. $1200.

1932, Rockwell. $800.

1933, Stanley. $850.

1934, Rockwell. $800.

1935, Rockwell. $800.

1936, N.C. Wyeth. $1200.

1937, Wyeth. $850.

1938. $800.

1939. $650.

1940. $650.

1941. $500.

1942. $450.

1943. $600.

1944. $400.

1945. $400.

1947. $400.

1951. $250.

1948. $450.

1949. $350.

1950. $300.

40

1957. $200.

1952. $200.

1953. $200.

1954. $250.

1955, Spanish. $250.

1955. $200.

1957. $250.

1958. $235.

1959. $175.

1961. $110.

1962. $100.

1963. $100.

1964. $95.

1965. $90.

1966. $90.

1968. $85.

1969. $85.

1970. $30.

1971. $35.

1971. $35.

1971. $30.

1972. $30.

1972. $30.

1973. $30.

1974. $30.

1975. $25.

1976. $20.

1978. $20.

1979. $20.

1980. $20.

1982. $15.

1983. $15.

1985. $15.

1972, linen. $25.

1973, linen. $25.

1974, linen. $25.

1977, paper. $15.

1973, Valentine reproduction of 1899 calendar. $25.

1976, paper. $15.

Heavy metal perpetual desk calendar. $200.

1927, Gardner Bros. Bottlers, Green Castle, IN. $125.

1974-1975, 12-sided plastic calendar. $25.

Pocket calendars. $3 ea.

1970s, perpetual calendar. $35.

1950s, calendar holder. $375.

44

BOY SCOUT CALENDARS

1947, boy scout, Rockwell. $550.

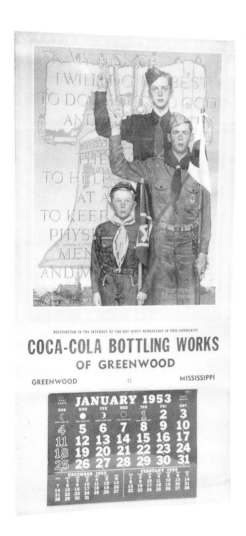

1953, boy scout, Rockwell. $475.

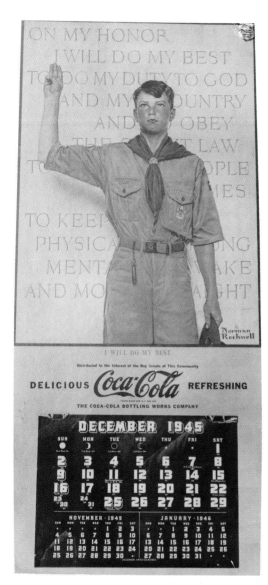

1945, boy scout, Rockwell. $500.

1946, boy scout, Rockwell. $500.

1939, 12 calendar girls, "The Girl on the Calendar Through the Years," 27-1/2" x 56". $850.

REFERENCE OR AT-HOME CALENDARS

1954. $40.

1955. $40.

1956. $40.

1957. $40.

1958. $35.

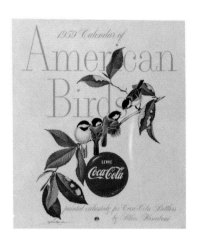

1959. $35.

1960. $35.

1961. $35.

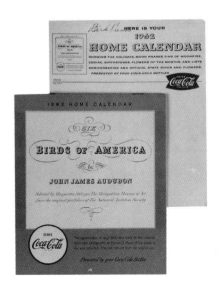

1962. $35.

1964. $35.

1965. $35.

1968. $35.

1969. $30.

1970. $25.

1975. $5.

1946, Sprite Boy, rare. $750.

1964, from Hong Kong, rare. $450.

CLOCKS

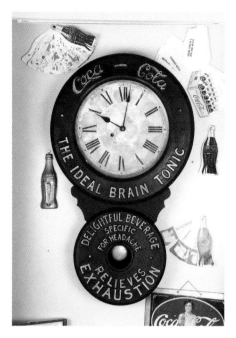

1891-1895, Baird clock, figure-8 version, papier-maché from the Plattsburg Era, labelled "Delightful Beverage." $5000.

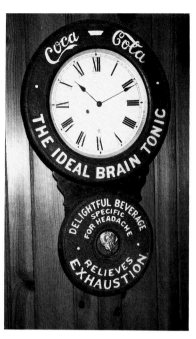

1891-1895, same as photo on left except face is better. $5000.

1910 GILBERT REGULATOR

1910, Gilbert Regulator clock, with decal of girl at base of clock. $2800.

1920s, Gilbert Regulator clock. $2000.

1920s, Gilbert Regulator clock. $2800.

1930s, silhouette clock, pulsating, 18" diameter, very rare. $2800.

1930s, silhouette clock with a metal frame, 18" diameter. $850.

1930s, octagonal neon silhouette clock. $1400.

1930s, wood-framed silhouette Selecto clock, 16" x 16". $500.

1930s, Seth Thomas white frame clock, rare. $850.

1939, wood-framed Selecto clock, 16" x 16". $425.

1950s, round silver tin clock. $210.

1950s, lighted clock with silhouette bottle, red center with green border, 17". $450.

1950s, round brown tin clock. $200.

1960s, plastic clock, 16" x 16". $150.

1970, Swihart electric clock, 4" x 9", very rare. $300.

1960s, lighted fishtail clock. $250.

1960s, lighted clock with red bottom panel. $275.

1960s, lighted fishtail sign, green or white background. $175 ea.

1950s, Dome clock. $1100.

1974, plastic "Sprite Boy" clock. $75.

1972, plastic schoolhouse clock. $65.

1974, plastic "Betty" clock. $65.

1970s, can-shaped electric clock. $40.

1970s, plastic pocketwatch clock. $45.

1950s, brass "will return" sign, 6" x 6". $110.

1970s, plastic travel alarm, 4" x 4-1/2". $75.

1970s, plastic electric clock with white top. $75.

1960s, German brass travel clock, 3" x 3". $150.

STUFFED TOYS & DOLLS

1950s, original Coca-Cola Santa, black patent leather boots, Rushton, 16" high. $185.

1960s, first black Santa from Coca-Cola, Rushton. $350.

1960s, later Santa, white boots, 16" high, Rushton. $165.

1970s, Santa, white boots, Rushton, 16" high. $135.

1970s, black Santa, Rushton, 16" high. $275.

1986, stuffed doll for Coke promotion. $50.

1964, plush political dolls, Rushton, 14" tall. $200.

1950s, Buddy Lee doll, original uniform, 12". Plastic doll, $750; composition doll, $850. (Note: New uniforms appear on the market often, so BEWARE!)

PAPER SIGNS, ETC.

1920s, "Treat Yourself Right," with metal strip hangers at top and bottom edges, 12" x 20". $900.

1920s, "That taste good feeling," with top and bottom edge metal hanger stripe, 12" x 20". $950.

1901, "Hilda Clark" sign, 15" x 20". As is, $4500; if in mint condition, $8500.

1929, "Off to a fresh start," top and bottom metal strips, 10" x 30". $2500.

1920s, "An ice cold with a red hot," with top and bottom metal strip hangers, 10" x 30". $2500.

1950s, metal strips on four sides, 21" x 11". $350.

1970, Raquel Welch advertising her new Coca-Cola brand of jewelry: watch, belt, bracelet, ring, and scarf. $75.

1936, Chinatown, 14-1/2" x 22". $1500.

1949, Edgar Bergan & Charlie, 11" x 22". $250.

1920s die-cut Japanese lantern. $750.

TROLLEY SIGNS

From San Francisco's cable cars, to New York's electric trolleys, to the "Plain Street Cars" found only in the Mid West...Those people too young to have run for the last step, to have squeezed through the crowd with hope of finding a seat, to have been relegated to hanging from a leather noose (for the tall) or a handy gymnastic boost (for the short)...they missed being eyeball with a trolley sign! Over the years the pretty girls and movie stars they featured were replaced with cartoon characters, babies, foodstuffs, etc...and some with Coca-Cola.

1923, "Four Seasons." $2800.

1912, "Drink Coca-Cola." $3000.

1907, "Tired." $2800.

1914, "Delicious and Refreshing," bottle w/paper label. $3500.

1907, "Relieves Fatigue." $3500.

1908, "Five Cents." $2800.

1923, "Flapper Girl." $3500.

1927, "Good Company." $2800.

CHRISTMAS CARDS & SANTA MAGAZINE PICTURES

1960, from the Sundblom "Santa Collection," Coca-Cola Co. $25.

1974, Sundblom Santa. $15.

1980, Sundblom Santa. $15.

1988, Christmas ball, Germany. $8.

1940, Marlinton, WV, Coca-Cola Bottling Co. $15.

1962, Sundblom Santa collection. $15.

1989, Gilles Collomb's Museum, Caluire, France. $12.

1950s, Springfield Bottling Coca-Cola Co., OH. $12.

1980s, Coca-Cola U.S.A. $8.

1976, "Silver Medallion" card, Sisterville Coca-Cola Co., West Virginia. $60.

1987, Coca-Col Collector from Holland. $8.

1989, Coke Collector card, Tokyo, Japan. $8.

CHRISTMAS MAGAZINE ADS, ETC.

1955. $20.

1962. $25.

1932. $20.

1961. $20.

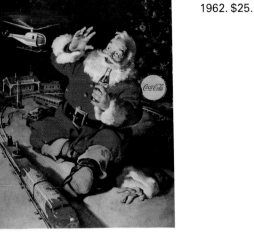

1965. $15.

1949, Santa and the Sprite Boy. $25.

1952, front of illustrated, striped card. $20.

Reverse of 1952 striped card, with "Twas the Night before Christmas" poem.

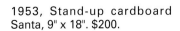

1953, Stand-up cardboard Santa, 9" x 18". $200.

SANTA CLAUS

1936, the first Santa used on the Cola Call.

1931, Santa, first one used by Coca-Cola Co.

In 1930, the Coca-Cola Company hired the well known artist Haddon Sundblom to create a realistic - human-looking Santa to use for their Christmas ads. The ugly, squeaky-voiced being of tradition disappeared! Sundblom did not have to search long or far to find a model for the new Santa Claus. Looking in the mirror at the wrinkles and dimples wrought his own Nordic face. Sundblom decided to pose for his Santa himself. In 1930 the first Santa appeared on his first Coca-Cola ad - gently plump, with twinkling eyes, plenty of wrinkles - and surely a robust voice to hearld in his "Ho, Ho, Ho" for the next 35 years Sundblom's different Santas became a continuing tradition. Haddon Sundblom died on March 12, 1976. WHAT A GIFT HE LEFT FOR SANTA LOVERS AROUND THE WORLD!

Sandblom & Santa.

(NOTE THE STRIKING RESEMBLANCE BETWEEN SUNBLOM AND HIS SANTA)

1905, pepsin gum jar with square corners. $900.

1905, Coca-Cola chewing gum jar. $900.

1910-1915, chewing gum shipping box, 12-1/2" x 6-1/4". $450.

(top) 1910-1920, pack wrapper for wintergreen Pepsin. $475.
(center) 1910-1920, spearmint wrapper. $400.
(bottom) 1910-1920, wintergreen wrapper. $400.

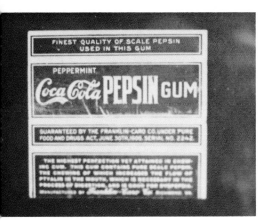

Peppermint wrapper. $500.

SCHOOL ITEMS

1928, Book of ABCs. $55.

1931, writing tablet with Rockwell cover illustration. $40.

1950s, comic book history of Coca-Cola. $20.

1950s, Old Chips and Charlie book. $20.

1970s, FDA regulations. $15.

1971, "Jr. Scholastic" magazine. $12.

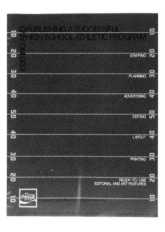

1970, A instructional guide for publishing programs for athletic events. $15.

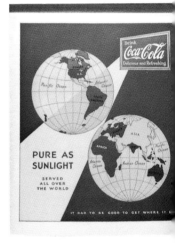

1930s, writing tablet. $30.

1930s, school tablet. $25.

1949, Sprite Boy. $25.

1940s, Sprite Boy and measurement chart. $25.

1960s, "Landmarks of the USA" tablet with Sprite Boy inside cover. $20.

1960s, U.N. flags on a horizontal tablet, with Sprite Boy inside cover. $15.

1960s, vertical school tablet with Sprite Boy inside cover. $15.

1970s, school tablet, Atlanta. $15.

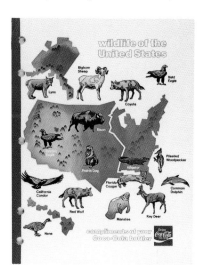

1970s, school tablet. $15.

1970s, school tablet. $15.

1970s, school tablet. $15.

1940s, schoolbook cover. $15.

1940s, schoolbook cover. $15.

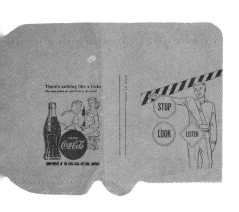

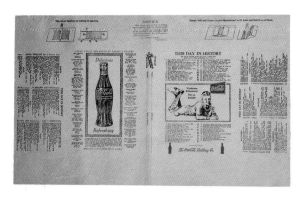

1930, schoolbook cover. $20.

1937, schoolbook cover. $20.

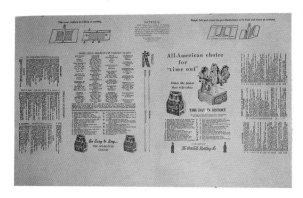

1940, schoolbook cover. $20.

1940s, book cover with Sprite Boy. $25.

1950s, book cover. $20.

1960s, book cover. $20.

1970s, book cover. $15.

Book cover. $25.

1942, book on coal from "Our America" series, with stamps. $20.

1942, "Our America" book about electricity, with stamps. $20.

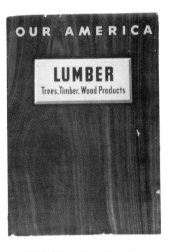

1942, "Our America" lumber book, with stamps. $20.

1942, "Our America" book on a motion pictures, with stamps. $20.

1942, "Our America" steel book, with stamps. $20.

Complete set of Nature study cards, 8 different packets with 12 cards each 2-1/2" x 4". $60.

1950s, "African Flowers" set, 100 illustrated cards, 2-1/2" x 4". $75.

1930s, cast iron pencil sharpener, Bavaria. $40.
Box of 12 complete with box. $500.

1950s, plastic pencil sharpener. $20.
1960s, plastic pencil sharpener. $20.
1950s, plastic pencil sharpener. $25.
1960s, plastic pencil sharpener. $25.

1950s, pencil clips. $10 each.

1930s, pencil boxes in two styles, each complete with 10 items. $55.

1950s, complete package of school items. $35.

1950s, complete package of school items. $85.

1970s, ball point pen. $10.

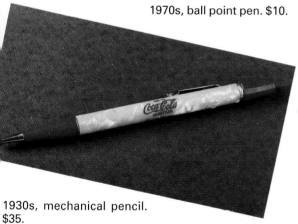

1930s, mechanical pencil. $35.

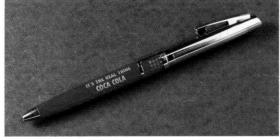

1970s, wooden baseball bat pencil. $15.

1930s, mechanical pencil with bottle. $85.

1970s, ball point with calendar. $50.

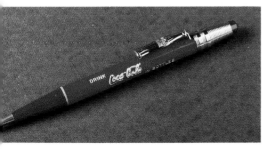

1950s, mechanical pencil. $40.

1960s, mechanical pencil. $25.

1970s, pen and pencil set with box. $50.

1960s, pen and pencil set with box. $60.

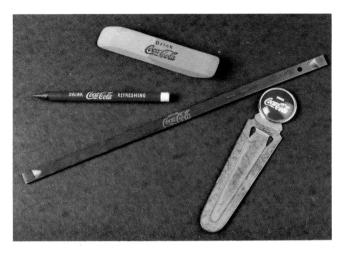

1960s, eraser. $10.
1930s, pencil slate. $35.
1950s, 6" brass ruler. $35.
1960s, book mark. $10.

Foreign lead pencil. $15.
1970s, lead pencil. $3.
1950s, lead pencil. $6.
1930s, lead pencil. $8.

1960s, truck sign for school safety, 66-1/2" x 32-1/2". $375.

1930s, lead pencil. $8.
1930s, lead pencil. $12.
1970s, lead pencil. $3.
1950s, lead pencil. $3.

1950s, set of four funny face pencils, Piqua, OH. $25.

1960, original pencil urn with dull finish, 7-1/4" tall, M.I.B. $275.

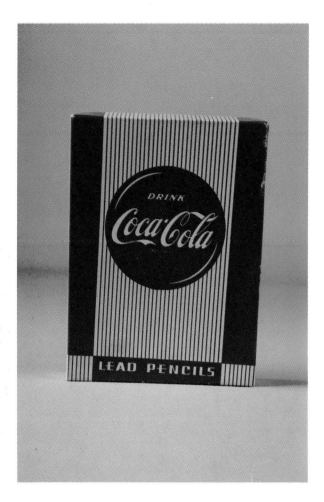

1950s, box of six dozen pencils. $250.

1970s, N.Y., 75th Anniversary replica of an original pencil urn, M.I.B., glaze finish, 7" tall. $125.

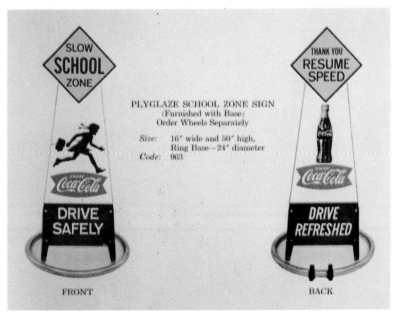

1960s, signs for the front and back of school zones, 24" base x 50" height. $600.

PENNANTS, BANNERS & UMBRELLAS

1940s, oil cloth, 30" x 50". $250.

1940s, burlap, 29" x 66". $300.

1970s, Hebrew, 60" x 40". $125.

1970s, notorious "Cocaine" banner using the Coca-Cola wave design. Coca-Cola Co. disapproved and the sign disappeared quickly. $150.

1915, framed, felt, in honor of General Nathaniel Greene and the soldiers who fought at the Battle of Guilford Court House. "Drink Coco-Cola from the bottle" is printed at the bottom. 18" x 30", rare. $600.

1940s, felt, 18" x 30". $350.

1930s, beach umbrella. $1000.

1960s, cardboard for schedule. $25.

1960, basketball streamer, 10" x 18". $30.

1960s, cardboard for schedule. $30.

1930s, 16" masonite/metal swimming sign. $350.

1958, cardboard poster, 16" x 27". $400.

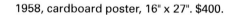

1960s, cardboard for schedule. $25.

1907, baseball ad, massengale. $125.

1939, "100 Years of Baseball," front. $325.

1939, "100 Years of Baseball," back. $325.

1960s, cardboard for schedule. $20.

1960s, cardboard for schedule. $25.

1936, program/score card. $35.

1961, batting & bunting. $25.

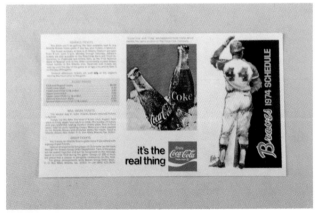

1980s, Braves schedule. $10.

1907, back of a perpetual counter, made of celluloid. $150.

1907, front of celluloid perpetual counter. $150.

1950s, score sheet. $10.

1980s, four different promotional balls. $10 ea.

1960, Ball of Fame, National League. $150.

1960, Ball of Fame, American League. $150.

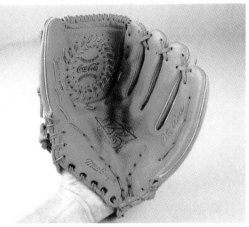

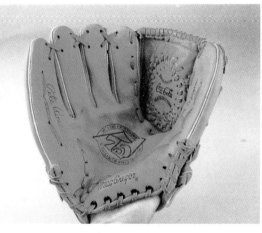

1976, left hand glove signed by Pete Rose & Joe Morgan. $250.

1987, glove signed by Johnny Bench. $250.

1976, right hand glove signed by Pete Rose & Joe Morgan. $250.

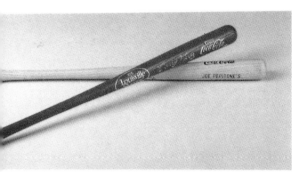

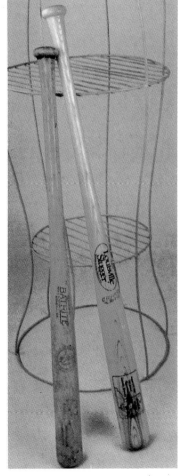

1987, Tony Perez mini-bat. $25.
1970, Joe Pepitone mini-bat. $40.

1981, Topps cards. $35 set.

(left) 1960s, "Batrite" bat. $85.
(right) 1990, Louisville National Convention bat. $30.

1982, Cincinnati Reds. $20 set.

1981, Kansas City Royals Topps cards. $10 set.

1950s, metal golf sign. $300.

1930, celluloid caddie badge. $175.

1960s, greens keeper, metal/case. $30.

Assorted golf balls. $15.
Plastic holder. $15.

1950s, three books of Stop-Action golf. $25 ea.

(left) Wooden golf tee. $8.
(center) Golf divot remover. $30.
(right) Golf ball marker. $80.

1950s, back of golf tee holder. $30.

1950s, front of golf tee holder. $30.

1960s, football. $25.

1960s, football. $25.

1960s, football. $25.

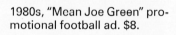

1950s, football. $30.

1980s, "Mean Joe Green" promotional football ad. $8.

1960s, football referee signs. $8.

1980s, Mean Joe Green
ad. $8.

1951, blotter. $50.

1960s, guide to basket-
ball referee signs. $8.

1932, Olympic disc. $225.

1932, reverse side of disc. $225.

1972, complete set of Olympic commemorative aluminum coins. $50.

1984, Olympic book. $30.

1984, calendar & note sheets. $15.

1960s, plastic bowling sign. $40.

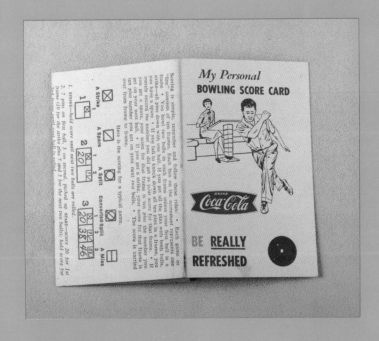

1960s, bowling score card. $30.

1960s, boating guide. $15.

1965, boating ad. $25.

1948, tennis ad. $25.

1960s, basketball. $25.

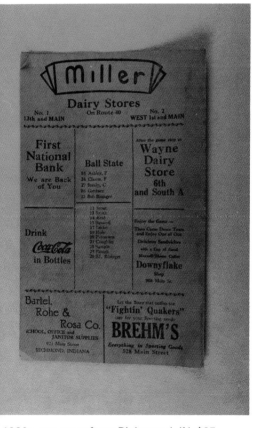

1930s, program from Richmond, IN. $25.

1955, sports manual. $40.

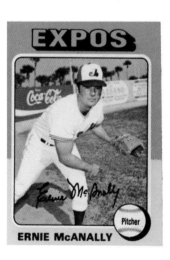

1980s, Ernie McAnally. $20 set.

1957, a calendar for special events. $8.

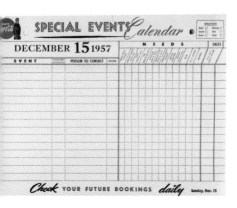

1960s, score-keeping card. $8.

PINS & JEWELRY

1-year pin, gold. $60.

5-year pin, one ruby. $85.

10-year pin, two pearls. $100.

15-year pin, three emeralds. $150.

20-year pin, four sapphires. $185.

25-year pin, five diamonds. $235.

30-year pin, six diamonds. $300.

45-year pin, nine diamonds. $525.

35-year pin, seven diamonds. $375.

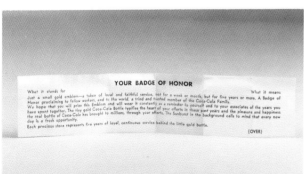

40-year pin, eight diamonds. $450.

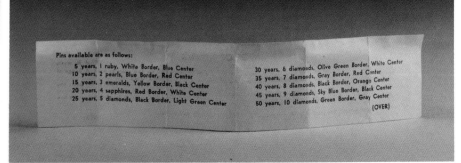

Information accompanying service pins.

1-year safe worker pin. $25.

7-year safe driver pin. $70.

1-year safe driver pin. $30.

5-year tie tack & clasp, one ruby. $85.

Set of sterling silver cuff links & tie clasp. $175 set.

1-year safe worker pin. $35.

1920s, celluloid cuff links. $125 pr.

1960s, tie clasp. $15.

1952, Fiftieth Anniversary money clip. $60.

1960s, tie clasps. $20 ea.

1960s, ring. $25.

1960s, tie clasps. $20 ea.

1950s, ladies' watch by Gruen. $500.

1950s, Eddie Fisher four-charm bracelet. $150.

1960s, NFL four-charm bracelet. $125.

1950s, sterling silver case to hold perfume bottle. $375.

1930s, glass perfume bottle, 3" tall with cap. $75.

1970s, two different service rings. $125 ea.

1960s, pillbox, 2-1/2". $30.

left to right:
1960s, wooden key chain. $15.
1950s, wooden key chain/flashlight. $30.
1950s, enamel/metal key chain. $35.
1960s, silver key chain. $60.
1960s, Pull-A-Part key chain. $30.

1960s, tape measure. $35.

1968, Indianapolis, IN. medallion $35.

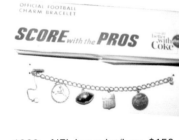

1960s, NFL bracelet/box. $150.

1986, Coca-Cola 100th Anniversary limited edition pin set. $375.

1986, Disney 15th Anniversary pin set, 60 pins. $375.

1985, Superbowl XIX pin set. $125.

LIGHTERS

1940, Bakelite ashtray with match-pull at top, rare. $1800.

1950s, Bakelite lighter and pen-holder. $150.

1962, gold stand-up Cygnus lighter. $175.

1970s, musical lighter. $275.

1950s, musical, blue bird. $300.

1950s, Coca-Cola. $85.

1960s, can with diamond-shaped pattern. $100.

1950s, Balboa. $65.

1950s, Handson. $65.

1950s, Perma-pic. $45.

1950s, Rosen-Nesor. $65.

1950s, 3-Lite. $125.

1970s, Cocaine. $90.

1950s, Rosen-Nesor. $125.

1950s, Dispos-A-Lite. $45.

1950s, Zippo. $100.

1950s, Zippo. $100.

1950s, Supreme. $40.

1960s. $45.

1970s, Chattanooga Plant. $50.

1970s, Park. $25.

1950s, pull apart. $60.

1960s, pull apart. $30.

1980, Prof-plastic. $25.

1960s, Scripto. (left) $75, (center) $75, (right) $85.

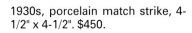

1930s, porcelain match strike, 4-1/2" x 4-1/2". $450.

ASHTRAYS

Pull-out cardboard ashtray for travel. $110.

1950s, tin. $25.

1970s, French glass ashtray. $15.

1936, porcelain, 50th Anniversary, Atlanta Biltmore Hotel, rare. $500.

With gold bottle lighter. $125.

1970s, punch-out bronze. $25.

1960s, Bakelite. $60.

1940s, Bakelite. $75.

1950s, Bakelite. $85.

1950s, tin. $35.

1950s, aluminum. $20 ea.

Tin from Mexico. $12.

Silvertone tin, from Mexico. $12.

1980s, red tin. $12.

1980s, tin. $12.

1960s, red tin. $12.

1960s, French metal ashtray. $25.

1970s, glass, in Spanish. $12.

1970s, glass, with labels in English (left and Spanish (right). $12 ea.

1950s, ruby-red glass set. $750.

1970s, Bakelite, French. $25.

1952, bronze-look anniversary ashtray. $75.

1936, frosted glass, 50th Anniversary cigarette box. $850.

COASTERS

0s, set of 4 aluminum. $18.

1960s, metal, given as an award. $25.

1950s, cardboard. $12.

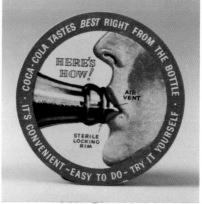

1950s, cardboard. $12.

50s, cardboard Sprite Boy. 5.

80s, set of 6, metal santas. 0.

1960s, boxed set of 4, cardboard. $20.

1960s, paper. $8.

70s, set of 4 plastic coasters in a box. $12.

1970s, set of 6, cardboard. $12.

1950s, cardboard. $12.

1940s, rubber, set of 4. $25.

1984, a set of 4 metal Coca-Cola girl coasters. $20.

81

CIGAR BANDS

Artemisa's Habana band in red, white & blue. $350.

C.E. Beck special. $300.

H.M.'s gold-embossed band. $300.

Red and green band, rare. $350.

1920s, Consolidated Litho Corp. $300 pr.

1933, page of bands showing the Coca-Cola band with bottle.

1933, Fortune magazine with a full page of cigar bands. $85.

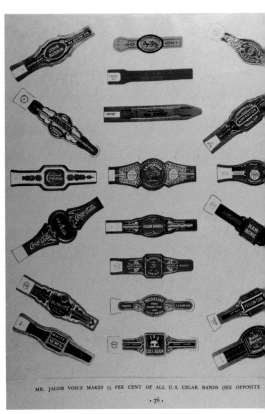

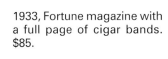

82

CARDBOARD SIGNS AND CUTOUTS

1934, Johnny Weissmuller & Maureen O'Sullivan, 14" x 30". $6500.

1944, set of 5 small-sized service girls, 17" tall. $2800.

1940, "Bather," 22" x 23". $1500.

1944, set of 5 Service Girls, 25" x 64", very rare. $5500.

1936, cardboard sign, 29" x 50". $1500.

1940s, "So Refreshing" poster, 16" x 27". $850.

1952, majorette, 20" x 36". $650.

1941, girl at cooler, 16" x 27", original frame. $800.

1936, bathers, 29" x 50". $5000.

1932, Claudette Colbert, 29" x 26". $6500.

1938, 30" x 50". $1800.

1923, picnic, 14" x 24". Printers Proof. $6500.

1932, 3-D pop-out sign, 10" x
20". $675.

1940s, "Carioca Cooler, sign with dangling bottles, 6" x 12". $1200.

1960s, The 3-D clown with jumbo-sized popcorn and Coke, 16" x 13". $150.

1950s, 16" x 24". $150 ea.

1955, skater, 20" x 36". $550.

1956, "Sprite Boy", 20" x 36". $475.

1960, a 3-D clown with popcorn and a Coke, 13" x 18". $125.

1960s, "Pause-Refresh" 3-D cutout sign with cup. $100.

1960s, "Pause-Refresh" 3-D cutout sign with bottle. $100.

1952, "Food Carousel," 16" x 20". $375.

1940s, "Soldier," 29" x 50". $1000.

1940s, "Boy and Girl at Fountain," 29" x 50". $1200.

1952, Fourth of July party, 30" x 50". $550.

1949, New Year's Eve party, 16" x 27". $950.

1952, "Girl with Dog," signed "Elvgren" by the artist at Edwards & Deutsch Litho Co. of Chicago. $850.

1934, Wallace Beery, 14" x 30". $1200.

1930s, "Skater and clown," 29" x 50". $1200.

1948, "Carousel," original frame, 30" x 50". $1800.

1930s, "Ballerina Circus Girl" window display cutout, part of 3-piece set. $4500 set.

1930s, "Clown" window display cutout from the 3-piece set.

1930s, "Ring Master" window display cutout from 3-piece set.

1950s, "Balancing Clown" cardboard, 5' tall, rare. $1000.

1931, "Uncle Remus" store or window display cutout, complete, rare. $5500.

1930s, soda fountain in 3 pieces. $6500.

1930s, large fire screen of heavy cardboard, very rare. $1800.

1930s, "Satisfy Hunger," 14" x 25". $975.

1920s, oval sign, 7" x 12". $750.

1920s, bottles from 1916 pictured in a metal-framed sign, 21" x 60". $1200.

1920s, die-cut cardboard wreath, rare. $1600.

1935, "Pause That Refreshes" sign, double-sided masonite, 21" x 13". $1500.

1936, 29" x 50". $2800.

1947, tennis girl, 16" x 17". $1000.

1939, "Think It's Swell," 20" x 36". $800.

1930s, "Hand with Bottle," 14" x 10".
$1250.

1940s, "Roller Skates," 16" x 27". $950.

1930s, rare advertisement, 9-1/2" x 11". $160.

1930s, rare advertisement, 11" x 14". $175.

1926, "Mrs. Wiggs of the Cabbage patch," 8" x 16", rare. The movie featured W.C. Fields, Zasu Pitts, Pauline Lords, and Evelyn Venable. $1800.

1930s, rare advertising poster, 11" x 14". $200.

1957, "58 million a day" Coca-Cola card, 16" x 27". $125.

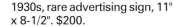

1930s, rare advertising sign, 11" x 8-1/2". $200.

1954, "Wheelbarrow Party," 16" x 27". $550.

1950, "Skiers," 20" x 36". $650.

1954, "Cooler Party," 20" x 36", original frame. $550.

1942, 29" x 50". $1250.

1940s, 29" x 50". $850.

1952, Oriental girl, 20" x 29". $550.

1930s, 27" x 56". $1800.

1956, Sprite Boy sign for king-size Coke, 20" x 36". $450.

1927, hanging sign, "7 million a day." $1200.

1960, snow streamers card, 11" x 17". $40.

1930s, "Refresh Yourself," double-sided masonite, 13" x 21". $900.

1960s, cold bottle display, 11-1/2" x 16-1/2". $100.

1943, "Girl with Coke," 16" x 27", original frame. $950.

1950s, two-sided board, 16" x 27". $850.

1954, "Coke Time", original frame. $750.

1950s, cutout, stand-up cardboard doll, 4" x 9-1/2". $750.

1960s, 3-D clown on a candy train, 14" x 18". $150.

1960s, 3-D bottle topper or dangler for king-size bottle. $35.

1960, "Spaceman" ad for king size bottle, 14-3/8" x 11-3/8". $125.

1960, one of a series of "Safety Cards," 11-7/8" x 15". $25.

1960s, cardboard cut-out of girl with a six-pack, 31" x 60". $225.

1960s, hostess with dancing feet, on a motorized cardboard display, approximately 32-1/2" x 13". $150.

1948, girl with ponytail, 30" x 50". $1250.

Reverse of 1950s board, 16" x 27". $750.

1960s, giraffe display for king-size bottle. $125.

1965, "Karry-Keg" ad featuring Anita Bryant, 19" x 24". $400.

1960s, two girls on a bike. $250.

1960s, two-sided cardboard snowman bottle display or dangler, 17-1/4" x 9-3/4". $100.

1950s, "Come Over For Coke, "20 x 36". $750.

1960, truck poster (enclosed) on truck frame, advertising "The Diamond Can," 22-1/2" x 66". $150.

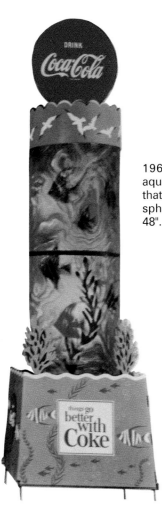

1960s, lighted cardboard aquarium sign, changing panels that create an underwater atmosphere, removable legs, 11" x 48". $750.

1960, another "Safety Card," 11-7/8" x 15". $25.

1952, cooler, 16" x 27". $550.

1940s, 21" x 11". $250.

1955, "Umbrella," 20" x 26". $650.

1930, bottle display cutout, 8-1/2" x 11". $850.

1944, "Lady Shopper" cutout with black hat, small size, 17-1/2" tall, rare. $475.

1930, 2-bottle display cutout, 8" x 11". $1200.

1944, "Lady Shopper" cutout with gray hat, large size, 62-1/2", very rare. $1200.

1927, "Toy Town" child's cutout gift, 10" x 15". $250.

1927, "Circus" child's cutout gift, 10" x 15". $200.

1929, "Corner Store" child's cutout gift, 10" x 15". $250.

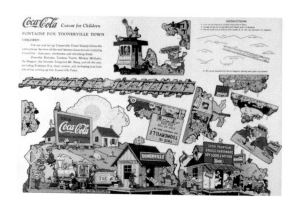

1930, "Toonerville Town" child's cutout gift, 10" x 15". $300.

1931, "Uncle Remus" child's cutout gift, 10" x 15". $450.

1932, "Olympic Games" child's cutout gift, 10" x 15". $275.

1932, "Circus" child's cutout gift, (glass), 10" x 15". $200.

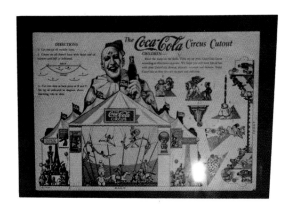

1932, "Circus" child's cutout gift, (bottle), 10" x 15". $200.

1940s, "Commando" soldier cutouts. $150.

1940s, commander of the "Commando" soldier game. $85.

1930s, five-color cardboard sign, 12" x 18". $150.

1920s, waxed cardboard sign, 10" x 14". $250.

FESTOONS

1918, "Parasols" theme festoon, with jointed sidepieces. $5500. In the original, these joints also bend the opposite way. Beware of reproductions, whose arms come together at the bottom.

1951, different faces from this back-bar display can be attached or separated. $1800.

1939, "Locket", with enlargement of the center. $1750.

1946, waitresses and Sprite Boy on a back-bar festoon, rare. $1500.

1939, "Jack-O-Lantern", scarce. $2800.

1932, "Verbena". $1500.

1951, "Refreshment through the years". $900.

1950s, Birthstones festoon. $900.

SALESMAN SAMPLE COOLERS

1929, Glascock single case cooler, 5-1/2" x 5-1/2" x 20-1/2", rare. As is, 7500; if mint, with original carrying case, $13,000.

1929, Glascock miniature double case cooler with bottles, 8" x 10" x 13", rare. As is, $6500; if in mint condition with original carrying case, $13,000.

1939, "Business builder" papers and insulation samples. $500.

(not pictured) 1939, closed front cooler with sliding panel to cover front, 8-1/2" x 11" x 9". $4300.

1939, "Open Front" complete with "business builder" papers, 8-1/2" x 11" x 9", rare. $4200 in mint condition.

PUSH-PULL PLATES

1950s, metal, 3" x 6". $250.

1950s, metal frame, plastic bottle. $285.

1930s, porcelain doorplate, 4" x 11-1/2". $300.

1930s, porcelain, 3-1/2" x 13-1/2". $325.

1930s, its porcelain mate, 4" x 11-1/2". $300.

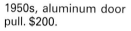

1950s, aluminum door pull. $200.

No. 101 All-Plastic Coca-Cola BOTTLE & BRACKET

1950s, plastic. $250.

1960s, metal, 4" x 8". $150.

1950s, porcelain push plate, 4" x 8". $300.

1950s, the matching pull, 4" x 8". $300.

(1) 1930s, porcelain, 1-1/4" x 35". $250.

(2) 1950s, porcelain, 3" x 32". $250.

(3) 1940s, porcelain with raised letter, 3" x 31-1/2". $250.

(4) 1950s, porcelain, 4" x 29-3/4". $250.

(5) 1940s, metal with silhouette, 3-1/2" x 33". $300.

(6) 1940s, porcelain with raised letters, 3" x 31-1/2". $275.

(7) 1930s, porcelain, 4" x 28". $275.

(8) 1950s, porcelain with raised letters, 3" x 40". $250.

CHINA & SILVERWARE

Taylor & Smith China. $275 ea.

1930s, ceramic snack bowl. $750.

1930s, sandwich plate from Knowles China Co., 7-1/4". $375.

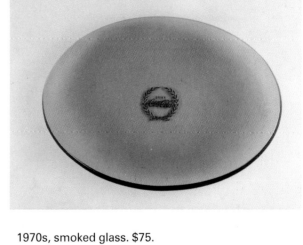

1970s, smoked glass. $75.

1960s, scalloped-edge world dish, 7-1/4". $125.

1960s, square world dish, 11-1/2" x 11-1/2". $125.

1970s, couroc plate. $75.

Silverware by Straus Co., Richmond, VA, Avon Plate & Wall Co.
$175 ea.

Coca-Cola logo on silverware handle.

1912, rice paper napkin.
$85.

1970, paper napkin. $5.

URNS

SYRUP DISPENSER - All original
Top and base marked "The Wheeling Pottery Co."
Two separate pieces - plus brass spigot

1896, syrup dispenser, original top & base marked "The Wheeling Pottery Co.", complete with lid, bowl and base, brass spigot 18" high. $5000.

1970s, white ceramic replica of original urn. $950.

1940s, rubber & plastic store display urn without a spigot; some one piece, others two pieces. $600.

1930s, advertisement for new type of frame. $500.

HABERDASHERY

1920s, soda jerk jacket. $175.
Linen soda jerk cap. $30.

1937, cowboy hat. $275.

1930s, apron. $40.

1940s, driver's caps with three different covers. $85 ea.

1930s, felt beanie caps, 8" diameter. $45 ea.

1950s, painter cap. $20.

1950s, baseball cap of wool and felt. $30.

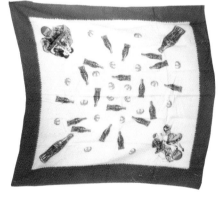

1950s, silk head scarf 34" x 34". $100.

1950s, Kit Carson kerchief, 20" x 22". $85.

1960s, soda jerk cap. $10.

1974, 75th Anniversary straw hat, Chattanooga, TN. $50.

1950 & 1960s, paper visor caps. $15 ea.

1920s, wooden pants hanger. $125.

NUDE LETTER OPENER

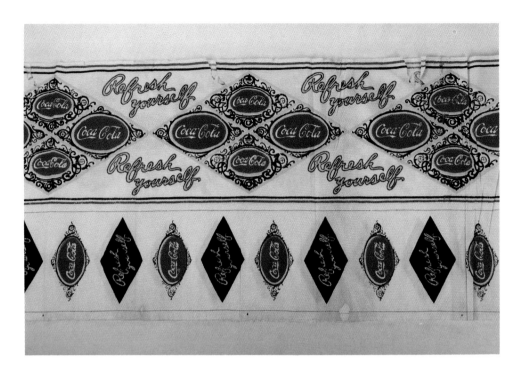

Crepe paper banner, 20' roll. $70.

Nude letter opener and its book-form box. $175.

Book-form box opened to show letter opener inside. Designed by Elvgren.

SEWING

1920s, chrome holder for thread, needles & thimble,
Coca-Cola Bottling Co. in San Antonio, TX. $150.

Thimbles:
(1) 1920s, red letters, "Drink in Bottles." $55.
(2) 1920s, in red letters, "Bottles" misspelled. $75.
(3) 1920s, blue letters, "Drink Coca-Cola." $90.
(4) 1920s, Thimble Whistle. $85.
(5) 1920s, word "Drink" only. $100.
(6) 1960, red & white plastic "Drink Coca-Cola." $25.

(left) 1924, needle case. $110.
(right) 1925, needle case. $90.

(left) 1970, sewing kit, complete. $8.
(right) 1970, Sprite Boy sewing kit in a metal tube.
$8.

W.W.II, (left) Navy sewing kit, complete. $45.
(center) Army sewing kit, complete. $45.
(right) Marines sewing kit, complete. $50.

PLAYING CARDS

1909. $2500.

1937, pinochle. $375 ea.

1938, pinochle. $275.

1938. $175.

1938. $175.

(left) 1943, regular cards. $175.
(center) 1943, Spotter cards. $150.
(right) 1943, Spotter cards. $150.

1915. $1800.

1938. $175 ea.

1943. $150 ea.

1943. $350 ea.

1928. $750 ea.

1938. $270 ea.

1938. $170 ea.

1940. $200.

1943. $350 ea.

1951. $110 ea.

1956. $110 ea.

1958. $100 ea.

1959. $100 ea.

1960. $100 ea.

1961. $100 ea.

(left) 1963. $85.
(right) 1963. $125.

1963. $80 ea.

1963. $60.

1965. $125.

1970, Waddington.
$175.

1971, Boy Scout, front and back. $200.

1971, Mexico. $65.

1971. $30 ea.

1970s, Don Nelson of the Milwaukee
Bucks, front and back. $150.

(left) 1970s. $35.
(right) 1970s, canasta. $55.

1974. $25.

1930s, Cincinnati,
OH. $175.

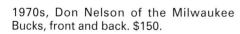

117

1974, gold box with small blocks. $25.

1974, gold box. $25.

1974, silver box. $25.

1974, large blocks. $25.

1970s. $25.

1976. $25.

1976. $45 ea.

(left) 1977, hard box. $50.
(right) 1977, soft box. $40.

(left) 1977, single deck. $30.
(right) 1977, boxed double deck. $60.

1979. $40 ea.

1979. $65.

1980, double deck. $65.

1979. $40 ea.

1979, double deck. $75.

1979. $40.

(left) 1979. $45.
(right) 1979. $35.

(left) 1980. $30.
(right) 1980, double deck. $55.

1980s, trivia. $20.

1980s. $10.

1980s, Spain. $60.

1980s, Belgium. $25.

1980s, Belgium. $20.

Campbellsville, KY. $60.

1978, Higeia, FL. $85.

1982, Kansas City, KS. $65.

(left) 1982. $45.
(right) 1982, double deck. $100.

1985. $25.

1985. $20.

1981. $40.

1987. $50.

1970, double deck. $45.

1980, double deck. $20.

1981, double deck. $20.

1986. $25.

1980s, double deck. $30.

1980s, classic. $40.

1983, New England. $60.

1988, Jeffersonville, IN. $65.

1988, Atlanta, GA. $35.

1939, Galesburg, IL. $175.

1930s, Galesburg, IL. $400.

1930s, Cincinnati, OH. $175.

1943, double deck and packet. $300.

CARDS FROM NATIONAL & MINI-CONVENTIONS

1988, "The Great Get Together." $45.

1991, "The Great Get Together." $25.

1992, "The Great Get Together." $25.

1987, E-Town, KY. $40.

1988, E-Town, KY. $35.

1989, E-Town, KY. $30.

1990, E-Town, KY. $25.

1991, E-Town, KY. $20.

1984, Zanesville, OH. $50.

1986, Zanesville, OH. $40.

1988, Zanesville, OH. $35.

1989, Zanesville, OH. $30.

1990, Zanesville, OH. $25.

1991, Zanesville, OH. $25.

1992, Zanesville, OH. $25.

1984, Sacramento, CA. $40.

1978, San Diego, CA. $40.

1980, Alexandria, MN. $165.

1985, Cola Clan. $45.

1986, Atlanta, GA. $40.

1989, Anaheim, CA. $40.

1992, Springtime Express, Atlanta, GA. $35.

1990, Louisville, KY. $25.

1992, Scottsdale, AZ. $25.

1991, Midsouth. $30.

121

BOOKS AND MAGAZINES

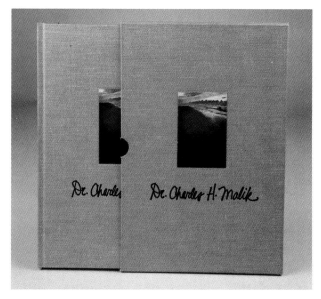

1972, Dr. Charles H. Malik, philosopher, wrote for Coca-Cola officers. $50.

1985, "Boss Emeritus" (Woodruff). $50.

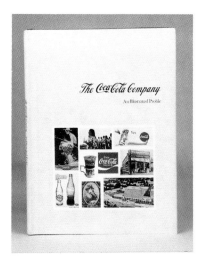

1974. $40.

Two portraits of the Coca-Cola business, with a chronological history. $10 ea.

One book................ $3 - $6.

Each bound book......... $10+

Complete set of 62...... $300+

Bound PAUSE books. There are 62 single copies, from the years 1954, 1969 and 1970. Most years had 4 issues: Autumn, Winter, Spring and Summer. A complete set is rare - it took us 7 years to complete our set. The first copy was and is still hard to find.

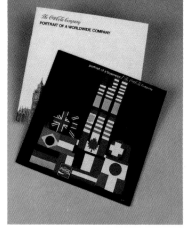

$10 each.

1886, three 100th Anniversary chronicles of Coca-Cola. $20 ea.

$15 each.

Whether you are a serious collector or a casual browser, xerox the chart below and carry it with you. It is a complete checklist of all the "Pause for Living" magazines issued over the years. Good hunting!

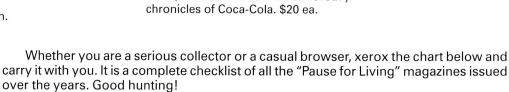

__ Autumn, 1954	__ Winter, 1958	__ Spring, 1963	__ Summer, 1967
__ Winter, 1954	__ Spring, 1959	__ Summer, 1963	__ Autumn, 1967
__ Spring, 1955	__ Summer, 1959	__ Autumn, 1963	__ Winter, 1967-68
__ Summer, 1955	__ Autumn, 1959	__ Winter, 1963-64	__ Spring, 1968
__ Autumn, 1955	__ Winter, 1959-60	__ Spring, 1964	__ Summer, 1968
__ Winter, 1955	__ Spring, 1960	__ Summer, 1964	__ Autumn, 1968
__ Spring, 1956	__ Summer, 1960	__ Autumn, 1964	__ Winter, 1968-69
__ Summer, 1956	__ Autumn, 1960	__ Winter, 1964-65	__ Spring, 1969
__ Autumn, 1956	__ Winter, 1960-61	__ Spring, 1965	__ Summer, 1969
__ Winter, 1956	__ Spring, 1961	__ Summer, 1965	__ Autumn, 1969
__ Spring, 1957	__ Summer, 1961	__ Autumn, 1965	__ Winter, 1969-70
__ Summer, 1957	__ Autumn, 1961	__ Winter, 1965-66	
__ Autumn, 1957	__ Winter, 1961-62	__ Spring, 1966	TOTAL 62
__ Winter, 1957	__ Spring, 1962	__ Summer, 1966	
__ Spring, 1958	__ Summer, 1962	__ Autumn, 1966	
__ Summer, 1958	__ Autumn, 1962	__ Winter, 1966-67	
__ Autumn, 1958	__ Winter, 1962-63	__ Spring, 1967	

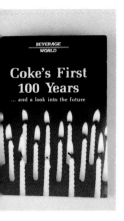
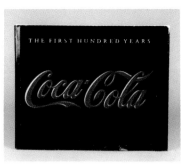
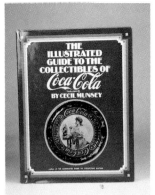

1986. $50.

1986. $100.

1972, by Cecil Munsey. $100.

1960, by Thomas Oliver. $25.

1940. $30.

1978, by Pat Watters. $25.

"The Big Drink," by E.J. Kahn, Jr. $30 ea.

1962. $30.

1983, Coca-Cola's Schmidt Museum book. $30.

1942, three books about flower arranging (Burrough). $10 ea.

1952, 50th Anniversary. $25.

Commemorative 50th anniversary portraits. $50 ea.

1976, Cincinnati. $15.

1916. $50.

1980s. $10.

1960s & 1970s, Golden Legacy. $8 ea.

1949, salesman training route book. $60.

1930, canasta pad. $35.

1940s, bridge pad. $35.

1940s, bridge pad. $40.

1943, bridge pad. $35.

1943, bridge pad. $35.

1944, bridge pad. $40.

(from left to right):
1940s, tally. $35.
1930s, tally. $45.
1930s, tally. $35.
1940s, tally. $30.

1952, Pam, bottle in center, 12" dia. $500.

1950s, Pam, fishtail dial, 12" dia. $450.

1950s, "Drink" by Robertson, 12" dia. $200.

1950s, "Drink in Bottles" by Robertson, 12" dia. $200.

1950s, "Sign of Good Taste" by Robertson, 12" dia. $200.

1960s, "Things Go Better" by Robertson, 12" dia. $225.

1970s, "Enjoy," 12" dia. $200.

1960s, "Things Go Better," 18" dia. $275.

1970s, "Enjoy," 18" dia. $275.

1915, wooden, 5" x 21". $800.

1905, wooden, 5" x 21". $750.
Smaller version (not pictured), 4" x 15". $675.

1950s, 30" long. $400.

1940s, porcelain, 8" x 36", very rare. $500.

1915, wooden, 5" x 21". $700.

1950s, 30" long. $350.

1920s, tin, Christmas bottle shape, 17". $300.

1930s, Christmas bottle shape, 17". $275.

1930s, 13". $100.

1940s, 17". $110.

1950s, 17". $100.

1950s, tin, 29" long. $250.

1950s, 17". $125.

1960s, 17". $45.

1956, 7-1/2". $40.

1950s, C-only, 7-1/2". $40.

1940s, Hund & Eger glass dome, 3", rare. $250.

1981, metal, Septemberfest, 13". $30.

1980, cardboard Sprite Boy, 9-1/2" tall. $25.

1980s, Mexican, 17". $30.

1940s, Metal. $85.

1940s, Plastic. $50.

1930s, on cardboard, 9" x 12". $400.

1920s, framed, illustrated, 8" x 10". $125.

1939, Canadian porcelain, 5-3/4" x 18". $450.

1938, oval Christmas bottle, 6-3/4" x 16". $300.

1930s, 6-1/2" x 16". $450.

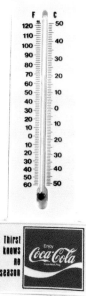

1970s, corner thermometer. $40.

1970s, plastic. $65.

1970s, plastic. $75.

1970s, plastic corner thermometer. $35.

1970s, plastic corner thermometer. $35.

1941, rare, silver-2 bottle. 7" x 16". $650.

1942, gold-2 bottle. 7" x 16". $600.

1945, masonite, 6-3/4" x 17". $450.

1970s, German "Trink." $30.

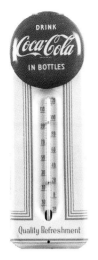

1950s, metal, 9". $175.

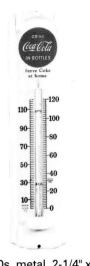

1940s, metal, 2-1/4" x 9". $200.

1960s, cardboard (Pre-mix), 6". $75.

1940s, Piqua Bottling Co. $20.

1970s, metal, Honeywell, 2" dia. $80.

1980s, 4". $30.

1960s, metal thermometer and pen holder. $25.

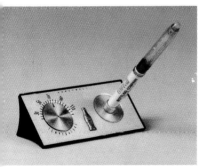

1960s, metal, 3-3/4" long. $75.

1940s, plastic, Piqua Bottling Co., 3-3/4" square. $50.

1960s, plastic thermometer, barometer and wind gauge. $100.

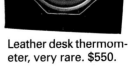

Leather desk thermometer, very rare. $550.

1926, 3-piece "Happy Thoughts" window display. $3500.

RADIOS

1931-1934, Bakelite Crosley radio from Cincinnati, functioning, 24" high, 7-1/2" diameter. $6500.

1949-1953, Bakelite Crosley Radio, "cooler" style, functioning. $900.

1970s, transistor, by J. Russell, M.I.B. $225.

1970s, AM/FM radio, plastic, functioning. $30.

1950s, transistor, functioning, 2-3/8" x 4-1/2". $250.

1950s, transistor, functioning. $250.

1950s, radio encased in red and white suitcase, rare. $1500.

1980s, transistor, functioning. $100.

1970s, AM/FM radio, M.I.B. $50.

1950s, crystal radio, plastic, parts complete. $350.

1960s, transistor, M.I.B. $250.

MINIATURES

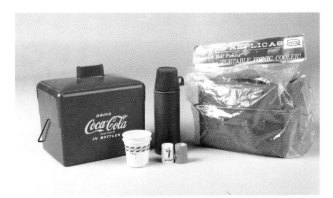

1950s, salesman's sample cooler with 2 different sets of items, 4" x 5" x 5". $175.

1950s, note pad holder with attached music box and pen. $300.

6-bottle packages (from left to right):
(1) 1950s, sectioned 6-pack. $75.
(2) 1970s, painted 6-pack. $25.
(3) 1970s, gold 6-pack. $30.
(4) 1970s, green 6-pack. $25.

1930s, wooden box, 24 bottles, 2-1/2" high. $300.

Display samples of 6-bottle packaging (from left to right):
(1) 1950s, enclosed box. $150.
(2) 1940s, 6-pack. $50.
(3) 1950s, curved novelty 6-pack from Bill's. $175.
(4) 1950s, sectioned 6-pack. $135.

1950s, cardboard miniature samples of in-store coolers. (left) $150, (right) $175.

1950, music box, plays Coca-Cola theme song and many other tunes. $225.

1950s, crystal radio, plastic, parts complete. $350.

1950, sales aide for distributors. $285.

1950, cooler with 6 bottles. $165.

Miniature Coke cases, each contains 24 1-1/2" tall bottles.
(right to left, starting on top row):
(1) 1960s, light green bottles. $35.
(2) 1970s, gold bottles. $30.
(3) 1970s, painted bottles. $25.
(4) 1960s, gold bottles. $35.
(5) 1960s, dark green bottles. $35.

1970s, plastic, Mexico, 2-3/4" bottles. $35.

PATCHES

Clockwise from left, then center:
(1) 1960s, "Things Go Better". $12.
(2) 1970s, "Coca-Cola" in Hebrew. $15.
(3) 1960s, 50th Anniversary. $25.
(4) 1980s, Navy Bee. $12.
(5) 1976, 75th Anniversary. $12.
(6) 1960s, fishtail-shaped. $18.
(7) Large white and red patch. $20.

(left) Red. $20.
(right) White.
$20.

(1) 1950s & '60s, "I Sell," large, red. $15.
(2) "Drink," large, red. $15.
(3) "Drink," large, white. $15.
(4) "Drink," small, white. $12.
(5) "Drink," small, red. $20.
(6) "I Sell," small, red. $15.

1904. $225.

1906. $150.

1906. $125.

1909. $175.

1909. $200.

1913. $40.

1913. $40.

1915. $100.

1923. $55.

1926. $35.

1927. $75.

1928. $90.

1929. $150.

1929. $150.

1929. $110.

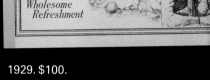

1929. $100.

1930. $85.

1930. $65.

1930. $110.

1930. $90.

1931. $140.

1931. $140.

1931. $110.

1932-33. $90.

1932-33. $135.

1932-33. $110.

1934. $100.

1934. $100.

1934. $100.

1934. $100.

1935, dated. $60.

1935, dated. $65.

1935, dated. $65.

1935, dated. $75.

1935, not dated. $50.

1935, not dated. $50.

1935, not dated. $50.

1935, not dated. $60.

1936. $75.

1937. $30.

1938. $25.

1939. $25.

1940. $75.

1941. $20.

1942. $20.

1944. $15.

1942. $15.

1947. $15.

1951. $20.

1951. $85.

1952. $90.

1953. $20.

1956. $15.

1957. $12.

1960. $12.

1940s. $25.

1942. $18.

1942. $18.

1937. $20.

1950s. $75.

1937. $20.

1938, Canada. $45.

1942, Spanish. $25.

1946, Canada. $45.

1948, Canada. $25.

1955, Canada. $30.

1950, Canada. $30.

1954, Canada. $25.

1954, Canada. $25.

Each blotter $35.

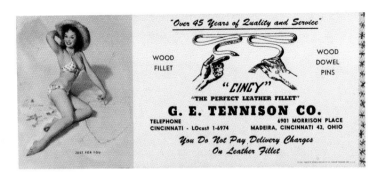

"Just for You."

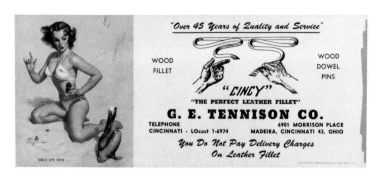

"Birds Eye View."

"Catering Wind."

"The Finishing Touch."

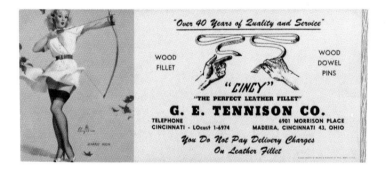

"Aiming High."

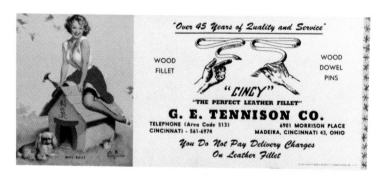

"Well Built."

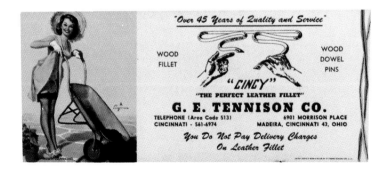

"Worth Cultivating."

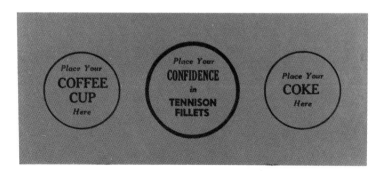

Back of Blotter.

Note: all of these Blotters (and many more) were drawn by the artist "Elvgren" (known for his Coca-Cola work and pretty girls).

CELLULOID

1930S, "Delicious & Refreshing" disc, Philadelphia Badge Co., 9". $350.

1940s, "Coke" disc, 9". $350.

1940s, "Delicious & Refreshing" disc, 9". $300.

1952, disc with 50th Anniversary disc. $425.

1950s, disc with bottle, 9". $200.

1942, celluloid over cardboard, Permanent Sign Co., 9". $950.

1942, celluloid over cardboard, Permanent Sign Co., 9". $950.

1903, note pad, 2-1/2" x 4-3/4". $700.

1902, stamp holder, 1-1/2" x 2-1/2". $650.

1930s, soap stone, 2-1/4" dia. $125.

SHADES

1930s, milk glass with fixtures, 14" diameter. $1500.

1920s, milk glass, 16" dia. $1250.

1920s, milk glass with porcelain fixture, 8" diameter. $850.

1920s, milk glass, 12" diameter. $1000.

1920s, leaded glass, band around tulips MUST read "Property of Coca-Cola," 18" diameter. $4800.

1920s, hanging, ball-shaped, leaded glass, 12" diameter, extremely rare: less than 10 known to exist. $9000.

1920s, milk glass lamp, embossed Coca-Cola on a metal base, 20" tall. $6500.

OPENERS & RELATED ITEMS

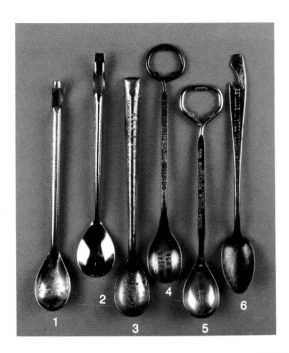

1920s & '30s
(1) "Drink Coca-Cola in Bottles" engraved in spoon opening, 7-3/4". $135.
(2) Coca-Cola Bottling Co., Greenwood, MS, 7-1/2". $115.
(3) By Hund & Eger, "Coca-Cola" written in spoon, 8". $230.
(4) "Happy Days" in spoon, Williamsport, PA, 8". $150.
(5) Clarksdale, MS, 7-3/4". $110.
(6) "Drink Coca-Cola in bottles" screw driver. $130.

(1) 1920s-1930s, Coca-Cola Bottling Co., Terre Haute, IN, 8-1/4". $130.
(2) 1920s-1930s, Coca-Cola Bottling Co., Milwaukee, WI, 7-3/4". $150.
(3) 1915-1930s, "Every bottle sterilized," 8-1/2". $150.

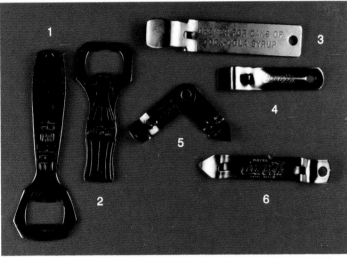

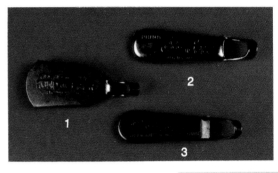

(1) 1930s, shoe horn, Coca-Cola Bottling Co., Waterloo, IA, 3-1/2". $285.
(2) 1930s, spatula, Coca-Cola Bottling Co., Greencastle, IN, 11-3/4". $260.

(1) 1950s, Coca-Cola & Schlitz, by Hund & Eger, St. Joseph, MO. $185.
(2) 1940s, Consolidated cork. $25.
(3) 1930s, Sesco. $40.

(1) 1950s, foreign. $60.
(2) 1950s, "Drink Coca-Cola". $30.
(3) 1940s, opener for syrup can. $45.
(4) 1950s, Walden cap opener. $30.
(5) 1960s, folding opener for bottles & cans. $25.
(6) 1960s, "Drink/Have a Coke." $25.

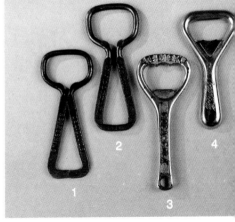

(1) "Refreshing - Delicious." $10.
(2) "Drink Coca-Cola in bottles". $10.
(3) 1910, cast iron. $140.
(4) German. $30.

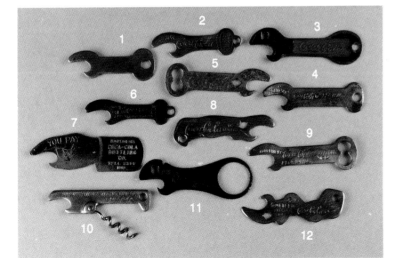

(1) 1930s, "Drink Coca-Cola". $40.
(2) 1930s, Vaughn style. $35.
(3) 1910-20s, red and black enamel. $110.
(4) 1920s, Springfield, OH. $45.
(5) 1915, skate key. $135.
(6) 1930s, spinner, Vaughn style. $135.
(7) 1915-20, spinner, hand style, Tell City, IN. $165.
(8) 1915, "Legs," bare with garter. $210.
(9) 1920s, Coca-Cola Bottling Co., Springfield, IL. $85.
(10) 1930s, Corkscrew, Coca-Cola Bottling Co., Enid, OK. $85.
(11) 1905-15, nail puller & cigar box cutter, "Delicious & Refreshing" on back. $85.
(12) 1915-30, Coca-Cola Bottling Co., Wichita, KS, nude on back. $200.

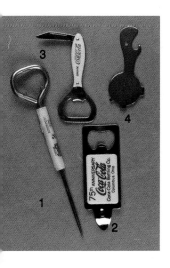

(1) Kingport, TN. $10.
(2) 1970s, Columbus, OH, 75th Anniversary. $20.
(3) 1960s, opener/knife. $20.
(4) 1970s, four-in-one turtle style. $12.

(left) 1980s, "Tome." $15.
(right) "Trink," German. $12.

1911-30, fish-shaped spinner. $200.

1960s, floating fish knife, wood and metal, 11". $35.

(1) 1950s, wall-mounted corkscrew. $55.
(2) 1925, wall-mounted corkscrew-hook. $80.
(3) 1925, Starr wall-mounted bottle opener. $85.
(4) 1920-1925, Starr. $15.
(5) 1920s, Protector Co. $160.
(6) 1920s, ball-cap or hoof shape. $120.
(7) 1970s, Starr-Beba. $15.
(8) 1950s, wall-mounted chrome. $30.

1960s, stainless opener for cans & bottles, 7-1/4". $30.

(left) 1950s, ice pick. $12.
(right) 1970s, "Tome" ice pick. $10.

1970s, Mexican ice pick/bottle openers. (left) $15, (right) $30.

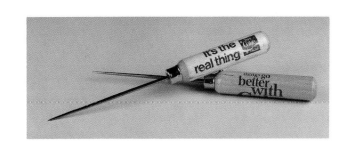

(left) 1970s, ice pick. $12.
(right) 1960s, ice pick. $15.

1950s, fly swatter, Helena, AR. $20.

German pull-apart corkscrew opener, brass, 5-1/2". $210.

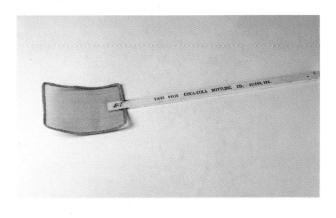

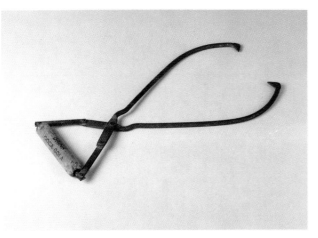

1920s, ice tongs - wooden handle. $300.

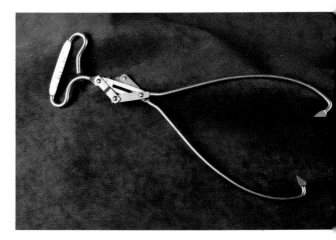

1930s, metal ice tongs. $250.

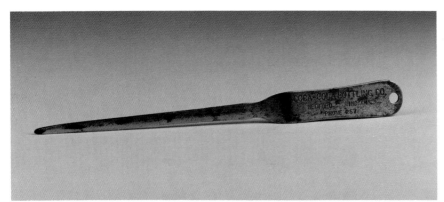

1920s, letter opener, Bedford, IN. $250.

1930s, pickle fork from Laurns Coca-Cola Bottling Co. $300.

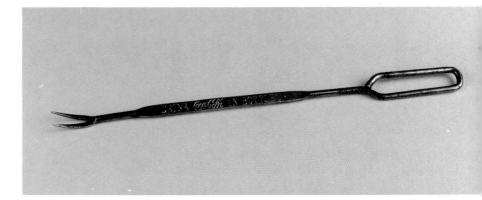

1970, stainless card suit openers, sleeve marked. $20 each.

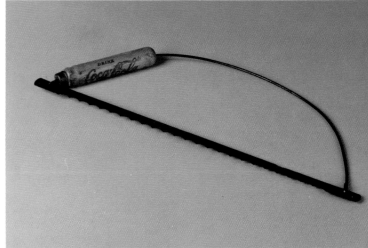

1930s, bread saw with wooden handle. $275.

FOBS

1. 1920 - Brass & red enamel - FOB. $175.
2. 1910 - Celluloid - "Drink Coca-Cola in Bottle" - 5¢ on back-FOB. $1000.
3. 1912 - Black enamel with brass - FOB. $200.
4. 1917 - Convention badge - metal disc on ribbon. $600.
5. 1910 - Celluloid "Drink Coca-Cola in bottles" - 5¢ on back. $1000.
6. 1910 - Girl FOB - back Memphis, Tenn. 5¢. $300.

1   2   3   4   5-top 6-bottom

Front

Back
left to right:
"Swastika," 1920s. $200.
"Drink Coca-Cola" in bottles 5¢, 1907. $200-brass.
bottom: "Drink Coca-Cola". Sold every 5¢, 1907. $200-silver.
top: "Drink Coca-Cola Delicious and Refreshing 5¢, 1920s. $200.

BOOKMARKS

1896, back 1892 2-sided celluloid bookmark, 2" x 2-1/4".
Complete, $900; single part $450.

1903, purple, 2" x 6". $500.

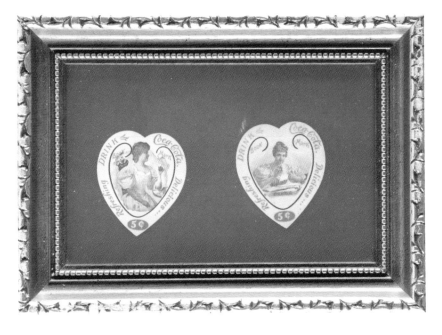

(left) 1898, celluloid, 2" x 2-1/4". $750.
(right) 1900, heart-shaped celluloid. $750.

(left) 1904, red, Lillian Nordica, 2" x 6". $450.
(center) 1905, green, 2-1/4" x 5-1/4". $550.
(right) 1906, celluloid owl, 1-1/2" x 3-1/8".
$850.

BANKS

1950, battery-operated, original box, 6-1/2" x 9-1/2". $600.

1950s, all-plastic, original box, 5-1/2" tall. $240.

1950s, translucent plastic, original box, 5-1/2", rare. $275.

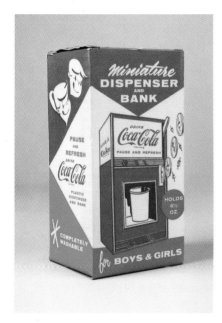

1950s, plastic bank, original box. $150.

1948, tin, 2-1/4" x 3". $150.

1960s, plastic, original box, 6". $75.

From Germany; one ad says "Trink Coca-Cola." $30.

1960s, plastic, 3". $15.

1960s, plastic. $25.

Tin bank, Coke logo on inside bottom. $60.

TOYS & GAMES

1940s, complete 6-piece game set, original box. $850.

1940s, 17-piece game set, M.I.B. $425.

1940s, table tennis game, M.I.B. $110.

1940s, bingo, M.I.B. $85.

1940s, tick tac toe set, M.I.B. $150.

1940s, Checkers / Acey-Ducey / Backgammon set, M.I.B. $165.

1960s, magic tricks, M.I.B. $150.

1940s, Dominos, bottle embossed on each piece, M.I.B. $60.

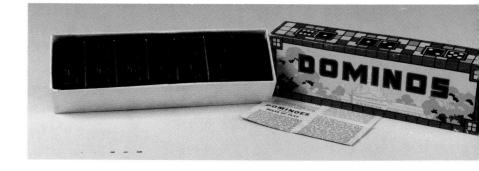

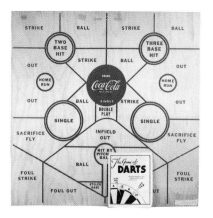

1940S, dart board. $125.

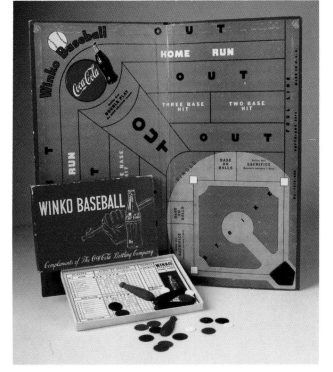

1940s, Winko Baseball board game, M.I.B. $300.

1940s, dart board. $125.

1938, Steps to Health game, complete. $85.

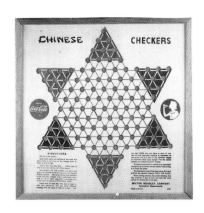

1940s, Chinese checkers board. $150.
1940s, checker board, obverse side. $150.

1930s, stick game. $100.

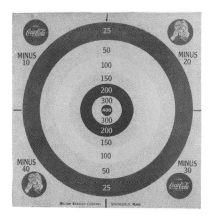

1940s, dart board, Sprite Boy. $150.

"Tower of Hannoi" games, very rare. $200.

1950s, "Shanghai" game, M.I.B. $30.

1950s, heavy cardboard toy shopping cart. $650.

1940/50s, glass fish bowl with paper label, filled with original chance tickets. $600.

1950s, bang gun with Santa. $20.

1930s, bang gun, Dayton, OH. $50.

1950, bang gun with clown. $25.

1930s, bang gun. Pure as Sunlight. $100.

1930s, jump-rope with whistle handle, "Pure as Sunlight." $375.

1930s, jump-rope, "Pure as Sunlight." $300.

1944, W.W.II puzzle, M.I.B. $125.

1944, photo of puzzle. $20.

1970s, cooler puzzle. $20.

1980, can puzzle. $20.

1980s, puzzle, M.I.B. $20.

1970, pop-art puzzle, M.I.B. $25.

1930s, dart board. $185.

1940s, horse race game, complete. $350.

1950s, toy Coke dispenser, complete, M.I.B. $150.

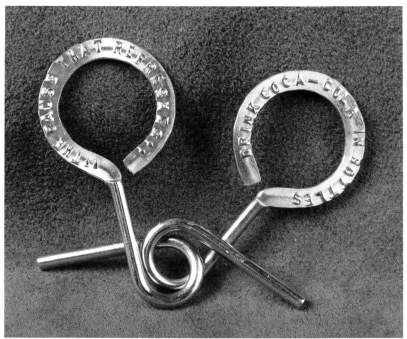

1950s, metal puzzle. $35.

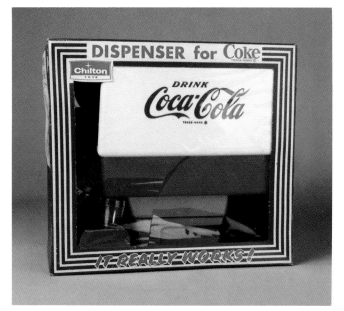

1960s, toy soda dispenser, M.I.B. $100.

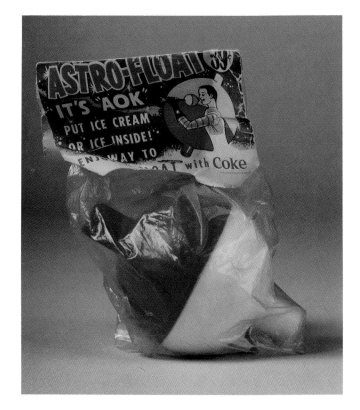

Astro-Float, sealed in package. $20.

1970, pop art checker, M.I.B. $50.

1930s, balsa wood hatchet, 12". $200.

1960s, wooden cap & ball game. $25.

1970s, frisbee, M.I.B. $30.

1970s, frisbee. $20.

1986, two dominos used in Britain's domino fall. $25 ea.

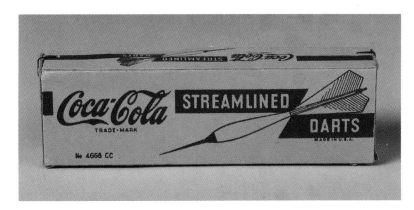

1950s, dart packaging with Coca-Cola logo. $85.

1950s, cap & ball game. $20.

1970s, wizzer for bicycle, M.I.B. $40.

1930s, wooden rabbit pull-toy, 3-3/4" x 4-3/4", very rare. $450.

Two-piece cardboard airport building. $225.

1974, wood & metal red wagon. $150.

1950s, tin "drive-in" model, 12" x 16", M.I.B. $300.

Bags of marbles. (left) 1940s, $60; (center) 1950s, $45; (right) 1950s, $35.

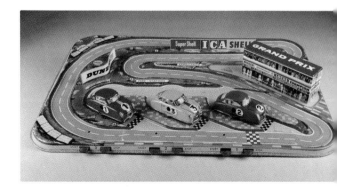

1950s, Grand Prix with 3 cars by Jim Technofix, 13" x 19". $200.

C. 1930, punch board, rare. $750.

1940s, punch board. $150.

C. 1930, punch board, 9-1/4" x 9-1/4", rare. $750.

1950s, wooden Playtown luncheonette, 7". $200.

1970s, Mexican dice game. $35.

Bingo cards. (left) 1930s, $40; (center) 1940s, $35; (right) 1980s, $20.

1940/50s, set of 14 plastic animals, each marked "Drink Coca-Cola", from South Africa. $200.

Logo on plastic animal from South Africa.

1936, magic lantern slides from Coca-Cola's 50th anniversary. $100 ea.

(left) 1970s, plastic spinning-top. $25.
(right) 1970s, plastic spinning-top. $25.

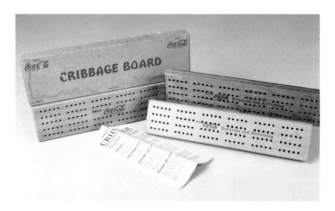

Cribbage boards, M.I.B. (left) 1940s, $90; (center) 1940s, $75; (right) $75.

1980s, Cobot, M.I.B. $175.

1930s, wooden yo-yo, Edwards Mfg Co., Cincinnati, OH, 1-3/4". $125.

1986, Coca-Cola Can Robot, M.I.B. $100.

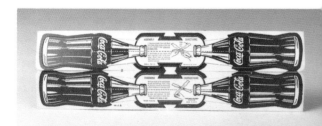

1950s, boomerang. $20.

(left) 1970s, Duncan Imperial yo-yo. $25.
(center) 1960s, plastic yo-yo. $35.
(right) 1970s, wooden yo-yo. $25.

1926, 3-piece "Happy Thoughts" window display. $3800.

LICENSE PLATES & BUMPER STICKERS

1940s, metal. $40.

1950s, metal. $35.

1970s, metal. $25.

1976, metal. $25.

1984, metal. $20.

1980s, miniatures. $10.

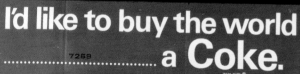

1960/70s. $5.

1960/70s. $5.

1960/70s. $5.

1960/70s. $5.

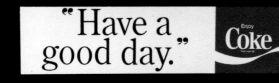

1960/70s. $5.

1960/70s. $5.

TRADE CARDS

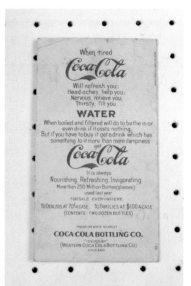

Back of metamorphic card.

1905, "metamorphic" trade card, folds to represent two different pictures, advertising on back, 5-1/2" x 6-1/2". $850.

1914, 3-D glasses (also called "verigraphs"), very rare. $750.

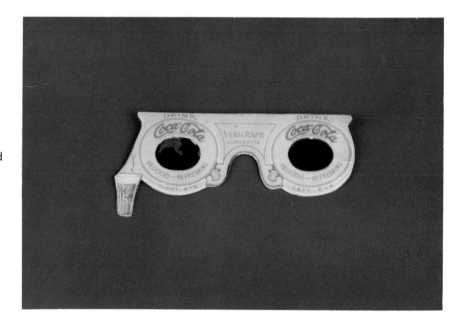

Cardboard sconce, 9" x 13". $500.

1978, original drawing by Bill Granstaff, "Keep Cool". $150.

OVAL MIRRORS

The following mirrors are 1-3/4" x 2-3/4" unless otherwise noted. The illustrations are covered by celluloid; the mirrors on the reverse are held by metal rims.

1922, mirror in great demand today, Whitehead & Hoag Co., Newark, NJ. $4200.

1906, by Whithead & Hoag, Newark, NJ. $800.

1920, Bastian Brothers, Rochester, NY. $1000.

1907, by Bastian Brothers. Rochester, N.Y., copyright by Wolf & Co. $800.

1916, Whitehead & Hoag Co., Newark, NJ. $600.

1911, "Duster Girl" mirror, also known as the "Motor Girl,: 1-5/8" x 2-3/8". All other mirrors were issued by Coca-Cola Co., but this one was put out independently by the Atlanta division; it is slightly smaller than the others. At the bottom it reads "Drink Coca-Cola in bottles," and the left rim reads "Cruver Mfg. Co." At most, 6 of these mirrors exist today. $5200.

1908, by Bastian Brothers, Rochester, NY. $2000.

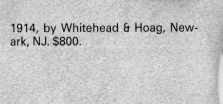

1914, by Whitehead & Hoag, Newark, NJ. $800.

1909, by J.B. Carroll, Chicago, IL. $800.

1911, Whitehead & Hoag, Newark, NJ. $600.

1910, J.B. Carroll, Chicago, IL. $600.

162

SPECIAL MIRRORS

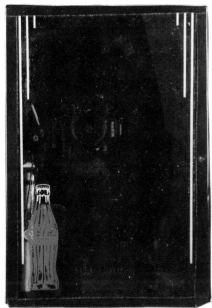

1920s, 10-1/4" x 14-1/2". $200.

1936, 50th Anniversary memo. $200.

1936, "Delicious & Refreshing" memo. $200.

1920s, folding cardboard cat from Germany, 2-1/2" x 2-1/2", rare. $550.

TRUCKS & CARS

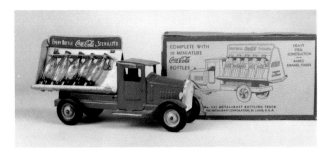

1930s, Metalcraft truck #171, rubber wheels, enamel finish and 10 miniature bottles, M.I.B. $1250.

1930, Metalcraft, metal wheels. $900.

1930, Metalcraft truck, rubber wheels. $950.

1930, Metalcraft, rubber wheels and working headlights. $1200.

1940s, "Smith Miller" truck, cargo of wooden blocks. $1250.

1940s, "Smith Miller," wooden blocks. $1100.

1950s, yellow metal A-frame, Marx. $850.

1950s, yellow metal, Sprite Boy. $650.

1950s, Sprite Boy, yellow, with red, white & blue detailing, M.I.B. $700.

1950s, Sprite Boy, red and yellow, M.I.B. $700.

1950s, yellow metal Marx, horn on top of the cab, M.I.B. $550.

1960, "Buddy L" truck, M.I.B. $450.

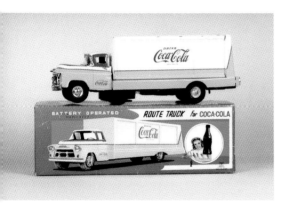

1950s, yellow and white, battery-operated, Haddock, M.I.B. $400.

1950s, battery-operated, Haddock, R & W, M.I.B. $475.

1950s, "Buddy L" loader. $450.

1950s, "Buddy L" flat top. $350.

1950s, yellow plastic. $300.

1960s, "Buddy L" plastic open-sided truck, 13" long. $450.

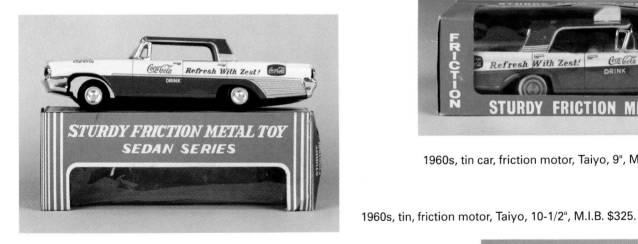

1949, plastic truck, Marx, 10-3/4", M.I.B. $450.

1949, plastic truck, Marx, 10-3/4", M.I.B. $400.

1960s, tin car, friction motor, Taiyo, 9", M.I.B. $400.

1960s, tin, friction motor, Taiyo, 10-1/2", M.I.B. $325.

1950s, Volkswagon truck, friction motor, by Taiyo, 8-1/2", M.I.B. $350.

1950s, tin delivery truck, friction motor, by Taiyo, 8-1/2", M.I.B. $375.

1950s, tin, friction motor, Rosko, 8", M.I.B. $700.

1973, "Big Wheel" trucks, Atlanta, New York, M.I.B. $90 ea.

1950s, Japanese friction, 3". $175.

1950s, yellow and red tin truck from Japan, 4-1/4". $175.

1960, pickup truck, 8" long. $650.

1970s, Smith Miller, M.I.B. $900.

950s, tin friction, pull-out bottles, 8-1/2". $800.

1950s, Japanese friction, tin, 5". $500.

1950s, tin, Volkswagon van, friction, 4". $350.

1940s, plastic, Pyro, 5-1/2". $150.

1970s, plastic, wind-up toy from Hong Kong, 3-1/2". $50.

1960s, plastic, Hong Kong, 4-1/2". $150.

1970s, plastic, wind-up circus engine, red and yellow top. $65.

1970s, plastic, wind-up circus engine, red & gold top. $75.

1970s, tin & plastic friction, Japan, 4-3/4". $80.

1970s, tractor trailer by Winross, M.I.B. $250.

1970s, tin & plastic friction, Japan, 4-3/4". $80.

1970s, SuperKings tractor trailer, M.I.B. $65.

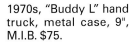

1970s, "Buddy L" hand truck, metal case, 9", M.I.B. $65.

1970s, "Buddy L" hand truck, metal case, 9", M.I.B. $75.

1979, delivery truck with Coke cases, 14", M.I.B. $50.

1979, "Buddy L" delivery truck with Coke cases, 7", M.I.B. $40.

1970s, two versions of one Coca-Cola truck, manufactured by two different Hong Kong companies, 5", M.I.B. $50 ea.

1977, plastic, Wee People from Straco in Hong Kong, 5-1/2". $50.

1970s, plastic "Cola Cars," black or orange wheels, 4", M.I.B. $35 ea.

1974, friction, Zip-A-Long from Hong Kong, 4-1/2". $50.

1970, "Buddy L" 5-piece set, M.I.B. $75.

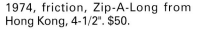

1970s, "Buddy L" racer, M.I.B. $75.

1950s, tin linemar friction, Japan, 2-3/4". $250.

1940s, two versions of a tin friction truck, Linemar, both 3-3/4". $250 ea.

1960s, cast iron, fishtail-shaped Coca-Cola sign, 2". $200.

1950s, Lesney's Matchbox Series: (left) Delivery truck, grey wheels, 2-1/2", M.I.B. $110.
(center) Delivery truck, irregularly staggered cases, 2-1/2", M.I.B. $125.
(right) Delivery truck, black wheels, 2-1/2", M.I.B. $110.

1978, Corgi-Met toy, 2-1/2", M.I.B. $20.

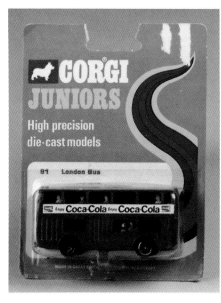

1973, Corgi-Met toy, 3", M.I.B. $25.

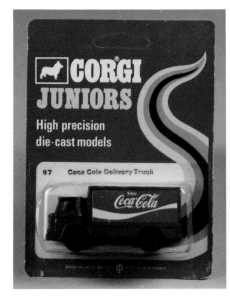

1973, Corgi-Met toy, 2-3/4", M.I.B. $20.

1976, plastic, Yat Ming, Hong Kong, 2-3/4", M.I.B. $15.

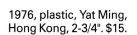

1976, plastic, Hong Kong, 2-3/4", M.I.B. $15.

1976, plastic, Yat Ming, Hong Kong, 2-3/4". $15.

1974, Zip-A-Longs from Hong Kong, 4 different styles, 4-1/2". $40 ea.

1978, Corgi-Met van, 4-1/2", M.I.B. $60.

1960s, plastic, Mercedes models, Germany, 1-5/8", M.I.B. $175.

1982, metal Corgi Pontiac/Firebird, 2-3/4". $35.

1980s, metal Siku Mercedes-Benz, 3-3/4". $45.

1970s, Pro Truck, M.I.B. $40.

1980s, metal Corgi Chevy/Corvette, 2-3/4". $30.

1978, Yesteryear Matchbox, 3-1/2", M.I.B. $75.

1970s, Japanese friction car, tin, 5". $35.

1940s, tin wind-up truck, Goso, U.S. Zone in Germany, 8-1/4", rare. $1850.

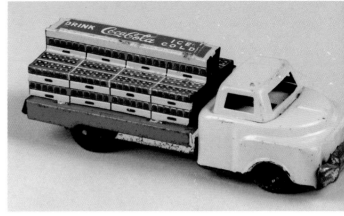

1950s, Japanese tin friction, 4-1/4". $700.

1950s, metal Bedford, Dinky, 4-1/2", M.I.B. $400.

1950s, Budgie Toys, 5-1/4", M.I.B. $375.

Die-cast Budgie V.W. pickup, 3-1/2". $50.

1980s, metal Dodge-Bache 4Y21, Solido, 4-1/4", M.I.B. $100.

1970s, red, metal, Renault, Solido, 3-1/2", M.I.B. $75.

1970s, yellow, metal, Renault, Solido, 3-1/4", M.I.B. $75.

1980s, two versions of metal Solido, Brumm, Italy. 3", M.I.B. $65 ea.

1980s, Solido metal Glamour, Italy, 4-1/2", M.I.B. $75.

VW-COCA COLA-Wagen   Batteriebetrieb

1970s, battery operated V.W. wagon, 4-1/2", M.I.B. $150.

1970s, plastic truck, Maxwell Calcutta, 3-3/8", M.I.B. $85.

1960s, by Berliet Stradair of France, 4-1/4". $350.

1980s, plastic truck from Germany, 5-1/4". $30.

1980s, Brooklin model of a 1936 Dodge Van, M.I.B. $150.

1970s, tin friction miniature, Japan, 2". $35.

Advertisement for Studebaker Coke truck. $50.

1970s, Bobby Allison kit for a 1/25 scale model, M.I.B. $135.

1970s, Model T van kit. $85.

1970, vending machine kit for a 1/25 scale model, M.I.B. $125.

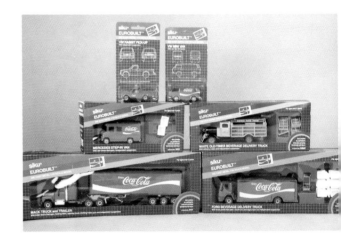

1980, set of 6 Siku Eurobuilts from West Germany, M.I.B. $200.

1970s, Athearn boxed car kit, M.I.B. $60.

1986, set of eight Days Gone models by Ledo, M.I.B. $200.

1980s, set of 8 Hard Toys from China. $100.

1981, in scale 1936 Ford panel truck, from the pewter nostalgic miniatures series, 4-1/8". $150.

1977, federal truck, pewter nostalgic miniatures, 2-3/4". $100.

1974, nostalgic miniature, Model-A-Ford, pewter, 3-1/4". $150.

1970s, nostalgic miniature, 3-1/2". $75.

1980, pewter Ram Cliffe truck. $50.

1974, nostalgic miniature Model-A-Truck, 3-1/2". $125.

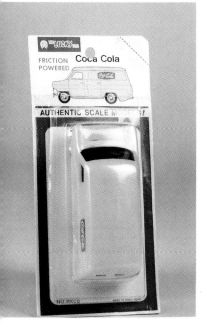

1980s, Lucky Toys friction truck, Hong Kong, 4-1/4". $50.

1970s, nostalgic miniature, 5-1/4". $125.

1970s, plastic Lapin truck, 11" x 18". $150.

1974, nostalgic miniature, Ford Model-A, 3-1/4". $125.

MASSENGALES & MAGAZINE PRINTS

1906, golfers. $75.

1907. $85.

1906. $85.

1904. $85.

1905. $110.

1905. $70.

1905. $85.

1910. $10.

1917. $25.

1912. $10.

1912. $20.

1914. $25.

1952. $15.

1919. $15.

1917. $20.

For the real times.

It's the real thing. Coke.

1975. $20.

1944. $15.

1929. $15.

So cool...so cooling

1937. $15.

1914. $15.

1948. $15.

1929. $15.

1915. $30.

1953. $20.

1916. $20.

1974. $20.

1943. $15.

1937. $15.

179

KNIVES

(front) C. 1910, Brass Kastor & Co. $400.
(back) Coca-Cola Bottling Co., Germany.

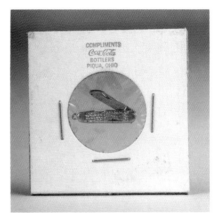

1960s, miniature metal knife from Piqua, OH, Coca-Cola bottling company. $30.

Front and back.

Front and back.

From the front:

(1) 1930s, Stainless A. Kastor & Bros. NY. $175.
(2) 1930s, Stainless Cutlery Co. NY, Coca-Cola Btlg. Co. $175.
(3) 1930s, Camilus New York, U.S.A. $150.

From the front:

(1) 1960s, Case NY., U.S.A. $75.
(2) 1920s, Bone A. Kastor & Co., NY. $175.
(3) 1970s, pearlized pin release for blade & opener. $60.

538
C. 1910, Brass Kastor & Co. $375.
539
C. 1910, silver, from D. Peres Solingen, Germany. $450.
542
C. 1920, bone, Kastor Bros. Coca-Cola Bottling Co. $200.
442
C. 1940, "Be Smart!" in window, Solingen, Germany. $225.
540
C. 1920, nickel/silver, D. Peres Solingen, Germany. $275.
456
C. 1910, key chain. $175.
543
C. 1920, "Jim Dandy" cigar cutter, screw driver, bottle opener, button hook. $325.

MISCELLANEOUS

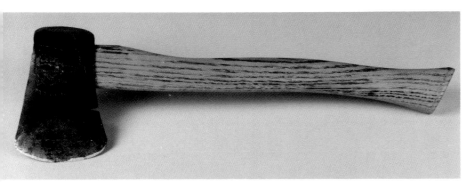

1930s, hatchet with metal head and wooden handle, 15". $350.

1970s, hatchet and a knife in adjoining leather cases, 10". $250.

1950s, magnifying glass with case. $30.

1970s, box cutter. $20.

1960s, manicure set in case. $25.

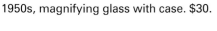

1960s, crate opener & nail puller from a Piqua, Ohio Bottling Co. $75.

1970s, first aid kit. $25.

1965, night light. $85.

1970s, sunglasses. $50.

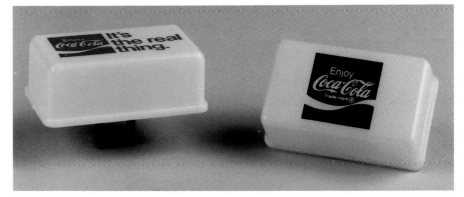

1970s, two night light styles. $35 ea.

1970s, night light. $60.

RARE SIGNS

1901, 6" dia., cardboard, bottom reads "Copyright 1901 by Coca-Cola Co." and "I Love The Flavor." Behind mirror is printed "Published by Wolf & Co., Philadelphia." Across top reads "Drink Carbonated Coca-Cola in Bottles, 5 cents." Extremely rare. $9000.

1916, "Elaine," hanging self-framed tin sign, 20" x 30-1/2". $7500.

1907, "Relieves Fatigue" self-framed tin sign, 20" x 30-1/2", rare. $10,000.

FURNITURE

1930s, Art Deco card table, 36" square. $250.

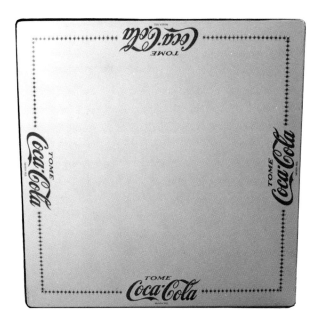

1950s, porcelain card table, 36" square. $200.

1950s, folding cardboard stadium seat. $50.

1970s, director's chair. $125.

1950s, metal folding chair. $100.

TRAINS

1930s, American Flyer train & track, engine stamped "AF 10," cars marked "American Flyer Line" & "Pure as Sunlight." If mint or near mint, $6500; individual car, mint or near-mint, $1250; with original box, add $600.

1974, Lionel transformer train set, M.I.B. $475.

The Lionel train.

1950s, tin wind-up double deck bus, track & terminal by Marke-Techno-FDC, Germany. Coca-Cola on small car. $450.

1960s, plastic box car, KMT, 10", M.I.B. $100.

980s, tank car, HO scale, 8". $35.

1970s, plastic box car, 10", M.I.B. $75.

1970s, box car and box, HO scale, 7". $90.

1970s, tank car, Tyco, HO scale, 8-1/4", M.I.B. $40.

1970s, tank car, Tyco, HO scale, 5", M.I.B. $35.

1970s, box car, Lima, Italy, 5", M.I.B. $40.

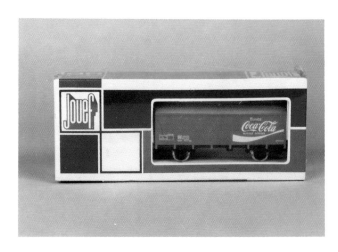

1970s, box car, Jouef, France, 4-1/4", M.I.B. $50.

1970s, box car, Lima, Italy, 2 x 3/4", M.I.B. $50.

1970s, box car, Lilliput, Austria, 4-1/2", M.I.B. $40.

1970s, box car, Fleischmann, 5-1/2". $50.

1970s, box car, Lilliput, Austria, 4-1/2". $50.

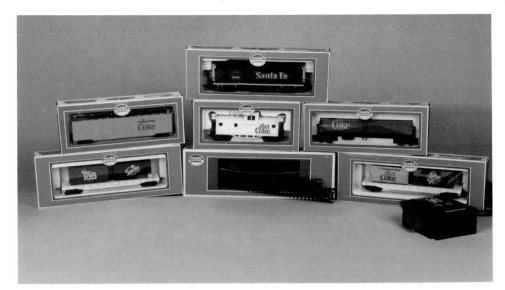

1985, model power train set, M.I.B. $140.

1970s, ROCO International, Austria, 5-1/2", M.I.B. $50.

1960s, two different billboards for train sets, 4" x 7". $40 ea.

1980s, Jolly Trolley from Hong Kong, M.I.B. $20.

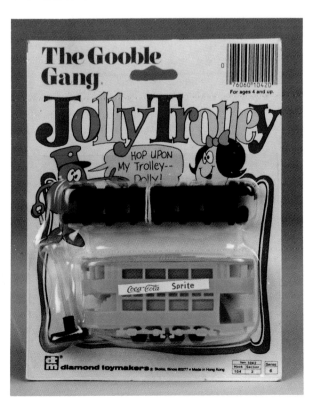

1970s, light-ups for trains, villages, and other model scenarios, 2" x 3-1/4". $25 ea.

FANS

1900s, front of bamboo fan. $200.

1900s, back of bamboo fan.

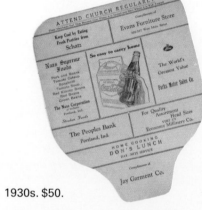

1920s, clown fan, opens and closes. $135.

1920s. $130.

1930s. $50.

1930s. $80.

1930s, rolled paper handle. $135.

1930s. $75.

1950s, wicker fan, Waycross Coca-Cola. $60.

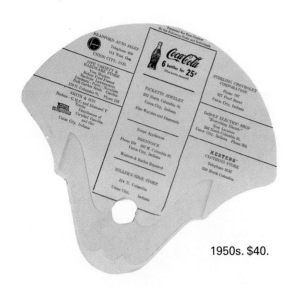

1950s. $40.

1950s. $60.

1950s. $65.

1950s, Sprite Boy. $60.

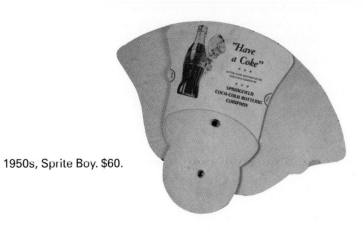

1950s, Sprite Boy. $60.

Plastic table mileage machine. $1200.

1960s, mileage chart, 8" diameter. $85.

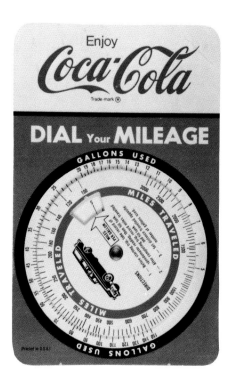

1970s, mileage meter. $15.

1938, road map. $25.

PAPERWEIGHTS

1950s, red & white glass by John Gentile, WV, 3-1/2" x 2-1/2". $150.

1970s, five-color by Gentile, 3-1/4" x 2-3/4". $75.

1970s, plastic, with bottle cap inside, 3" dia. $35.

1976, glass, from Coca-Cola's 90th anniversary, 3" x 4". $40.

1986, glass, from Coke's 100th Anniversary, 2-7/8" x 4". $85.

1970s, International bottle caps in lucite, 4-3/8" x 4". $55.

1974, marble and metal, anniversary weight from Chattanooga, 2-1/4" x 4-1/4". $75.

1974, lucite, 75th Anniversary, Chattanooga Bottling Co., 3-1/8" x 5". $45.

Note: The paperweights made by John Gentile were given to us by him. The multi-color is one of a kind - the red & white is one of several. I do not consider them WORTHLESS. He is famous in the paperweight world!

POSTCARDS

1910, Coca-Cola girl postcard by artist Hamilton King. $950.

1911, "Duster girl." $950.

1940s, Popeye, set of 4 with band, issued during W.W. II. $100.

1940s, Dick Tracy, set of 4 with band, issued during W.W. II. $100.

1940s, set of 4, Dick Tracy shows each; issued during W.W. II. $100.

1930s, Coca-Cola plant, Cincinnati, OH. $85.

1930s, Salida, CO. $35.

1930s, Grandad Minzey's Food Shop. $100.

1930s, 3 chain postcards, Dayton, Ohio. $85 ea.

International truck. $15.

1940s, Christmas postcard. $15.

1950s, Wilson's Grocery. $25.

1980s, London. $12.

1964, NY World's Fair. $12.

DECALS

1980s. $3.

1960s. $10.

1970s. $5.

1970s. $3.

1970s. $3.

1970s. $3.

$100.00 REWARD

1960s. $8.

things go better with Coke

1960. $5.

1970s. $3.

1980s. $5.

1950s. $15.

1960s. $10.

1950s. $15.

1970s. $5.

1960s. $12.

LIGHT PULLS

1960s. $65.

1950s, two-sided. $100.

1950s, two-sided. $90.

1950s, two-sided. $75.

1944, sign, 14" x 32". $750.

1950s, fan. $60.

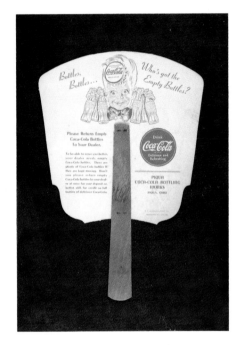

1950s, fan from Piqua, OH. $65.

1949, school tablet. $25.

1950s, coupon. $15.

1950s, paperweight. $25.

1964, program. $25.

1949, magazine ad. $35.

1950s, school tablet. $25.

1950s, coaster. $15.

Decal, 7-3/4" x 10". $40.

1950s, napkin. $15.

1950s, coaster. $15.

1950s, decal. $175.

1979, playing cards. $40.

1947, magazine ad. $35.

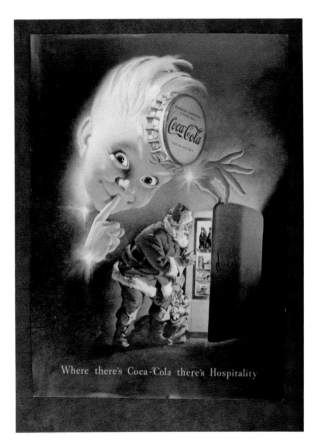

1950s, opener, M.I.B. $30.

1980s, thermometer. $25.

CONTINUOUS QUALITY IS QUALITY YOU TRUST

DRINK Coca-Cola "Coke"

1947, magazine ad. $35.

1970s, plastic dominoes. $25.

1940s, advertising layout. $50.

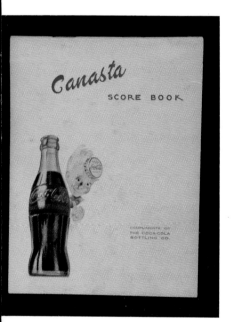

Canasta SCORE BOOK

1950s, canasta score pad. $35.

Take Home a Carton

1950s, decal, 8-1/4" x 10-1/2". $40.

1950s, German, glass, 9-3/4" dia. $700.

1950s, coupon. $15.

Have a Coke FREE when this card is presented at our fountain YOU'LL BE GLAD YOU DID

SOLE'S DRUG STORE
3060 Main St.
WEIRTON - Phone 3060

(Over)

1950s, napkin dispenser, rare. $850.

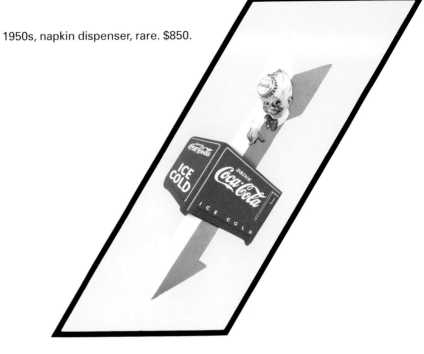

1940s, wooden arrow sign. $1000.

1975, *Cola Call* cover. $15.

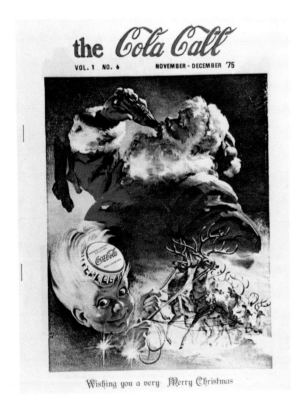

1982, tray from Nashville, TN. $75.

SPRITE BOY

ALL ABOUT A FANTASY

(Is It Worthless)

To Coca-Cola collectors, a "fantasy" is an item made up unofficially from odds and ends of other items — there is no original, "real" Coca-Cola piece like it. There are those collectors who call these pieces of "fantasy" worthless.

The item pictured is considered to be "fantasy" — but it is still made up of FOUR original Coca-Cola pieces! These are:

1. Center world with hand, from a 1956 blotter,
2. Center world with hand, from a 6" x 27" cardboard poster,
3. Girl skater, from a 1941 tray, and
4. Movie star Lupe Velez, from a stand-up cardboard.

These are four REAL, official pieces of Coca-Cola memorabilia, put together into one attractive sign. Some people call it a WORTHLESS fantasy — BUT IT IS NOT!

SIGNS - BOTTLE

1920s, tin, with November 16, 1915 bottle, 6" x 13". $1000.

1920s, Christmas bottle tin sign, 6" x 13". $650.

1930s, porcelain, 12-1/2". $250.

1932, tin embossed die-cut, 3'. $1100.

1940s, metal, 30". $250.

1940s, embossed tin, 17". $225.

1940s, embossed por-celain, 17". $300.

1940s, convex tin, 17", rare. $150.

1940s, tin, 8" x 30". $200.

1950s, plastic display, 20". $550.

Bottle frame for display, 16" x 42", rare. $950.

1950s, embossed masonite, 18" x 36". $225.

1950s, pressed wood, 6'. $350.

1950s, convex sign, 3' (pictured), $450; 6' version, $550; 9' version, $850; 12' version, $950.

1950s, plastic fits on top of bottle, complete. $650.

SIGNS - BUTTONS

16"

36"

24"

12"

All 1950s

Size	Description	Price
12" -	Drink - tin	$250
12" -	Drink in Bottles	$250
16" -	Drink - tin	$300
16" -	Drink in Bottles	$300
24" -	Bottle on front-porcelain	$400
24" -	Drink in Bottles	$350
24" -	Drink	$350
36" -	Drink - tin	$350
36" -	Drink in Bottles	$400
36" -	Bottle on front-porcelain	$500

SIGNS - GLASS

1950s, reverse-on-glass wall hanging, 8" diameter. $175.

1932, reverse-on-glass, fits back-bar mirrors, 11" diameter. $750.

1930s, metal trim & chain, by Burnnhoff, Cincinnati, OH, 11" x 31". $1200.

1950s, reverse-on-glass, wooden frame, Price Bros., Chicago, IL. 11" x 15". $650.

1950s, reverse-on-glass wall hanging, Price Bros., Chicago, IL, 12" x 18". $750.

1950s, reverse-on-glass, wood frame, fits on top of cash register, Price Bros., Chicago, 4" x 10-1/4". $575.

1920s, reverse-on-glass, 10-1/2" x 20", very rare. $800.

1950, reverse-on-glass, 6" x 22-1/2". $175.

1930s, reverse-on-glass, tin stand-up frame, 5" x 14". $600.

1950s, motion-lighted, 9" x 20". $800.

1950s, "Waterfall" cashier's sign, 9" x 20". $900.

1950s, square-faced clock, 9" x 20". $750.

1950s, clock, round face, 9" x 20". $600.

1950s, "Shop Refreshed," two-sided. $500.

1960s, stand-up, pulsating, 11" diameter. $600.

1950s, "Please Pay When Served" with white glass insert, 8" x 15". $650.

1950s, with red glass base, 8" x 15". $650.

1950s, "Please Pay When Served" ribbed glass front, 8" x 18". $500.

1950s, reverse-on-glass, metal frame, fits on cash register, 6" x 11". $500.

1950's Stand Up Lighted Sign 2 sided

Front & back:
1950s, stand-up, 2-sided. $575.

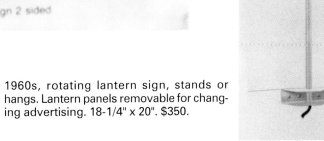

1960s, rotating lantern sign, stands or hangs. Lantern panels removable for changing advertising. 18-1/4" x 20". $350.

1930s, rolled-edge frame, 12" x 16", rare. $1250.

1920s, lighted bottle, red milk glass, embossed metal base, 20". $6500.

1960s, "The Shooting Star" motion sign; bottom panel remains lit at all times, 16" x 14-1/4". $450.

1940s, booth light with Sprite Boy. $200.

SIGNS - PORCELAIN

1926, with green trim, 10" x 30", rare. $900.

1932, five-color, 10" x 30". $900.

Five-color, 12" x 30". $550.

1920s, four-color, 12" x 31". $600.

1935, one-sided half-sided, 14" x 27". $850.

1930s, two-sided half-shield, 14" x 27". $1250.

1935, triangle, two-sided, bottle illustration. $5500.

1930s, "Fountain Service," two spigots, 14" x 27". $4000.

1935, shield-shaped, 22-3/4" x 25-1/2". $3000 if two-sided, $2500 if one-sided.

1950s, arrow sign, 12" x 28". $450.

1950, rolled ends, 18" x 54". $600.

1960s, rolled ends, 18" x 54". $475.

1930s, two-sided, 25" x 26". $950.

1950s, two-sided, 24" x 26". $950.

1950s, two-sided, 20" x 64". $700.

1940s, 24" x 24". $475.

1960s, flange sign, 17" x 19". $475.

1926, oval sign, 8" x 11". $3500.

1926, rectangular sign, manufactured by Tindeco, 8-1/2" x 20". $4000.

1927, manufactured by Tindeco, 8-1/2" x 11". $4000.

1931, manufactured by Tindeco, 8-1/2" x 11". $2000.

1910, 12" x 36". $2500.

1920s, flange, 11-5/8" x 16". $950.

1926, five-color, 12" x 35". $1500.

1927, two-sided arrow, 7-3/4" x 30". $1100.

1927, five-color, 10-1/2" x 31". $800.

1920, 6" x 22-1/2". $500.

1930s, five-color sign, 6" x 18". $475.

1931, embossed Christmas bottle, 4-1/2" x 12-1/2". $550.

1920s, Dasco, 5-3/4" x 17-3/4". $475.

1935, five-color, Christmas bottle, 12" x 36". $450.

1940s, two-sided, 9-1/2" x 15-1/2". $300.

1933, five-color, 19-1/2" dia. $750.

1932, five-color, 19-1/2" diameter. $800.

1950s, tin, 16-1/2" x 42", topped by a 16" disc. $1000.

1950s, six-pack sign, 11" x 12". $850.

1950s, six-pack sign, 11" x 12". $850.

1950s, arrow & bottle sign, 12" x 36". $350.

1950s, arrow & bottle sign, 20" x 28". $350.

1950s, movable arrow sign, 20" x 28". $350.

1960s, 12" x 36". $350 ea.

1950s, tire rack, 24" dia. $695.

1960s, five-color, 18" x 24", scarce. $200.

1960s, 11" x 28". $350.

1960s, fishtail, 18" x 54". $475.

1960s, two-sided, 11" x 30", rare. $575.

1960s, fishtail, 18" x 54". $350.

1950s, whirling sign. $750.

1960s, fishtail, 20" x 42". $400.

216

1950s, 10" x 28". $375.

1950s, aisle marker. $400.

1950s, six-pack sign, 30" x 36". $900.

1930s, tin kay display with a cardboard back. $675.

1940s, 20" x 28". $450.

1940s, 18" x 54". $450.

1940s, 20" x 28". $275.

1930s, 9" x 12". $550.

1930s, German flange, 18" x 24". $300.

1930s, 18" x 54". $475.

1940s, 18" x 34". $325.

1930s, embossed, 20" x 22-1/2". $300.

1940s, 9-1/2" x 22-1/2". $300.

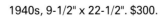

SIGNS - WOOD

1930s, two-piece kay display with bracket, 8" x 26". $750.

1940s, Sprite Boy masonite arrow. $1000.

1950s, masonite, 20" x 28". $475.

1950s, kay display with rope trim, 15" x 19". $775.

1940s, pressed wood, 4" x 8". $50.

1930s, triangle, applied wood bottle, one-sided. $750.

1930s, triangle, applied wood bottle, two-sided. $850.

1930s, triangle with metal trim, 19" edge. $1200.

1930s, with metal trim, applied wood bottle. $800.

1930s, kay display with metal trim, 12" x 22", rare. $1000.

1945, fiber-board, 13" diameter. $750.

1940s, bottle & horseshoe on wooden plank. $575.

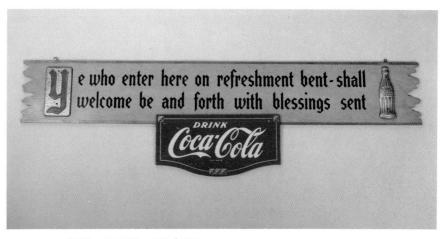

1930s, 10-1/2" x 39". $600.

1940s, with metal brackets, 9" x 36". $650.

1920s, with aluminum, bottle & arrow. $650.

1920s, chrome, for front of truck, 18". $450.

Cast aluminum, for top of truck cab. $850.

1930s, wooden scroll sign, 8" x 22", rare. $800.

C. 1920, porcelain, for front of truck. $750.

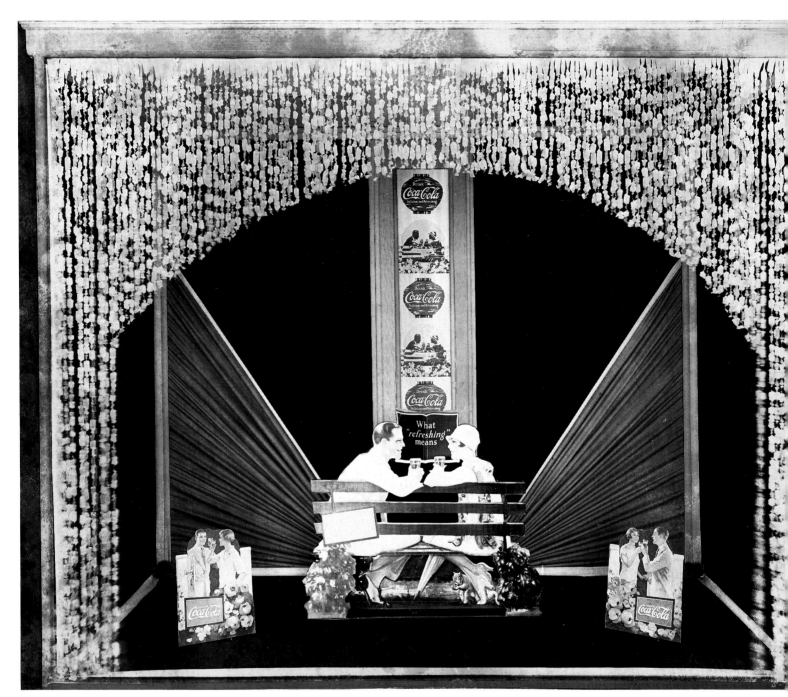

1928, elaborate 3-piece stage or window display bench scene. $2700.

COUPONS

Fronts

Backs

1908, front side of coupon, 1-5/8" x 3-3/8". $175.

1908, back of coupon.

1908, front of coupon, Colorado Drug Co., 1-5/8" x 3-3/8". $300.

1908, back of coupon.

1920s, front of rebate ticket, 1-1/4" x 2-1/2". $50.

1920s, back of rebate ticket.

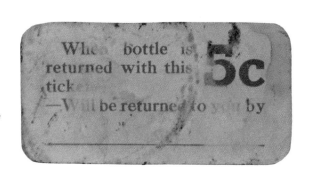

1924, front of coupon redeemable for silverware, from Ullrich Bottling Works in Lewistown, Pa., 2" x 3-1/2". $60.

1924, back of silverware coupon.

1920s, front of coupon, 1-1/2" x 2-3/4". $125.

1920s, back of coupon.

1920s, illustrated coupon, Thomas Bottling company, 2-1/2" x 3-1/2". $20.

1920s, back of illustrated coupon.

1935, coupon, N. Carolina, 2-3/8" x 4-1/4". $35.

1930s, coupon, 5-1/2" x 6-1/2". $15.

1930s, coupon, 5-1/2" x 6-1/2". $15.

1930s, coupon, Shelbyville, IN., 5-1/2" x 6-1/2". $15.

1930s, illustrated coupon, 2-1/2" x 5-1/4". $25.

1950s, coupon, Coke's 65th anniversary, 6-1/4" x 5-3/8". $15.

1920s, front of 5-cent coupon, 1-1/8" x 2". $50.

1950s, "direct mail" coupon, Coke's 65th anniversary, 5-1/2" x 3-1/4". $10.

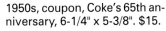

1930s, bottler's coupon, St. Louis, MO., 4" x 2-1/2". $8.

1958, 5-1/2" x 3-1/4". $10.

1950s, eleven coupons in book, 5" x 2". $10.

1950s, from Rockford, IL., 5-1/2" x 3-1/4". $8.

1950s, Piqua, OH., 3-3/4" x 2-1/2". $8.

1950s, Sprite Boy, 4-1/2" x 2-1/2". $15.

1950s, Piqua, OH., 6-1/4" x 3-1/4". $8.

1950s, Terre Haute, IN, 3-3/4" x 2-1/2". $8.

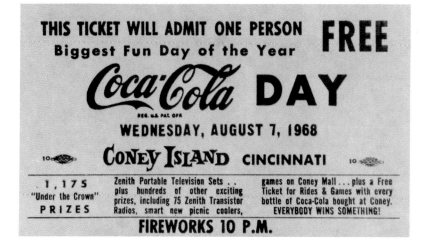

1968, carnival admission and raffle ticket, Coney Island, Cincy, OH, 4-3/4" x 2-1/4". $20.

1960s, Piqua, OH, 6-1/4" x 2-3/4". $8.

1963, King-Size Coke coupon, 6-1/8" x 2-3/4". $8.

1960, 6-1/8" x 2-5/8". $8.

1973, rum-and-Coke novelty coupon from Coca-Cola and Bacardi, 5" x 4". $8.

1970s, 5" x 2". $5.

1960s, Piqua district coupon, 6-1/4" x 2-3/4". $8.

1963, 3-5/8" x 2-1/8". $8.

1982, amusement park admission coupon, 1-3/4" x 3-1/2". $5.

1980s, 1-3/4" x 4". $5.

1980s, contest tag, 1-3/4" x 4". $5.

1964, coupon & program for Scottish Rite Christmas party, Cincinnati's Masonic Temple. $25.

Front of Lillian Nordica coupon.

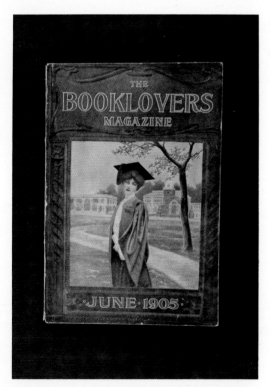

"The Booklovers Magazine," one of many periodicals in which a full-page Lillian Nordica illustrated coupon appeared. Full page with coupon, $275; magazine with coupon, $400.

Back of Lillian Nordica coupon.

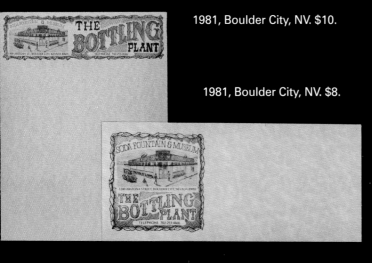

1981, Boulder City, NV. $10.

1969s, Cincinnati, OH. $7.

1981, Boulder City, NV. $8.

1950s, Ellensburg, WA. $4.

1976, 75th Anniversary envelope Cincinnati, OH. $5.

1940s, Winter Haven, FL. $10.

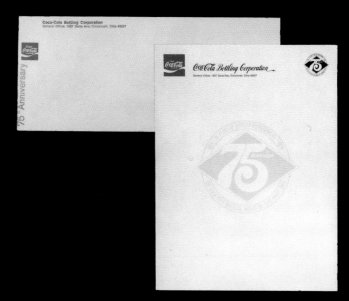

1940s, envelope from Winterhaven, FL. $4.

1976, Cincinnati, OH. $5.

1970s, Cincinnati, OH. $3.

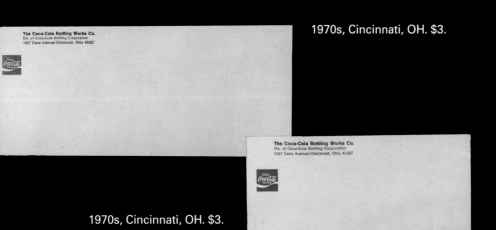

1970s, Cincinnati, OH. $3.

1920, envelope from Monroe, MI. $5.

1928, check from Santa Cruz, CA. $4.

1930s, letterhead, Piqua, OH. $10.

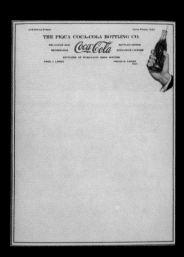

1955, check from Santa Cruz, CA. $3.

1960s, Ellensburg, WA. $8.

1960s, Ellensburg, WA. $8.

1976, Coca-Cola seal to Helen Wilson by Coca-Cola archivist William Kurtz. $10.

1938, Coca-Cola check, Santa Cruz, CA. $4.

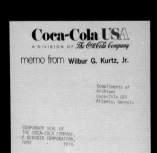

1972, Coca-Cola Seal. $8.

1976, Coca-Cola Seal given to Al Wilson by Kurtz. $10.

NOTEBOOKS

1903, leather notebook, gold lettering. $300.

1925, Webster's "Little Guy" Dictionary. $60.

1936, 50th Anniversary pocket secretary. $125.

1943. $15.

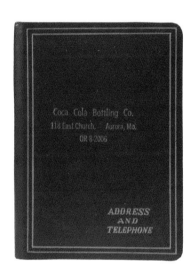

Telephone & address book. $30.

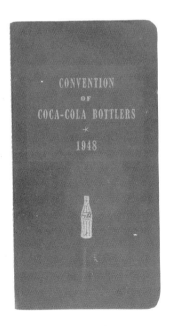

1948, Bottler's Convention. $40.

The 5th Ace. $15.

1960. $30.

AIRPLANES

1929, The Story of Aviation. $175.

1942, cardboard poster, 20" x 22". $60 ea.

1943, Know Your War Planes. $55.

1943, set of 20, in folder, 2" x 3". $125.

1941, cardboard, 20" x 22". $60 ea.

1943, cardboard, 13" x 15". $60 ea.

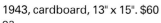

MISCELLANEOUS

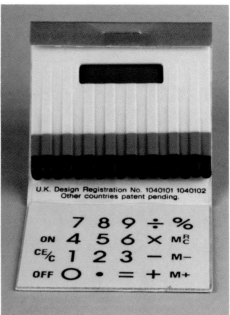

1980s, open calculator. $35.

1980s, closed calculator. $30.

1920s, notepad holder for telephone. $850.

1950, metal address
pad holder. $60.

1972, plastic calendar holder
to clip on phone. $15.

1965, plastic notepad
holder. $25.

STANDARDIZED DELIVERY EQUIPMENT

Coca-Cola made a great effort to control the uniformity of colors and design of equipment bearing the words Coca-Cola. These are examples of the exact painting and lettering specifications for each type of truck or auto. The panel style on each type of truck was also crucial.

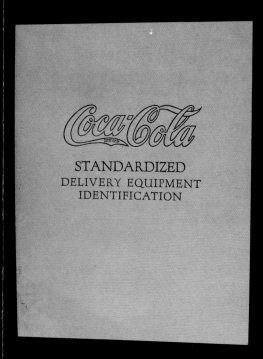

1931, complete "Standardization of Delivery Equipment" booklet with 24 written pages, including the cars shown here. $350.

Salesman's or service car.

Deck type of delivery truck.

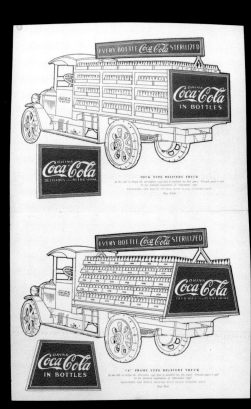

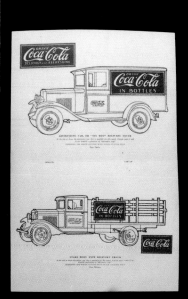

Advertising car or "Six Box" delivery truck.

"A" frame delivery truck.

Stake body delivery truck.

MISCELLANEOUS

Case Closed

1955, salesman's selling kit. $225.

1900, wooden dolly to carry barrel of syrup. Back reads "Howe Scale Co., Cincinnati, Ohio." "Every Where Coca-Cola in Bottles," rare. $1700.

1950s, salesman's training program, open & closed. $225.

Metal "Salesman of the Month" statuette, 6-1/2" tall. $750.

1920s, tin string holder, 16" high, rare. $850.

1930s, brass padlock, 1-1/2" x 1-1/2". $175.

1920s, door chain and lock, M.I.B. $75.

1920s, brass street marker, rare. $175.

BILLFOLDS

Most of these bill folds are leather.

1907. $200.

1910. $250.

1910. $150.

1912. $135.

1915. $100.

1912. $200.

1918. $125.

1919, with calendar & notebook. $125.

1920s, with 1916 embossed bottle. $75.

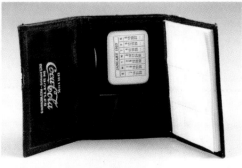

1923, with calendar. $100.

1915. $100.

Additional titles of the 1906 "Juanita" sheet music:
Lead Kindly Light
The Palms
My Old Kentucky Home
Rock Me To Sleep Mother
My Coca-Cola Bride
Old Folks at Home

1906, sheet music for "Ben Bolt," approximately 10" x 14". $950.

1927, music for "The Coca-Cola Girl." $375.

1927, sheet music for "The Coca-Cola Girl," 9-1/2" x 12-1/2". $375.

LEN JOY when he composed famous theme song.

"Coca-Cola Signature"
By Leonard W. Joy.

JOY MUSIC

Could you recognize the real Coca-Cola theme song?

Maybe not...
It has no name!
It was never played all the way through!
It was written as a tango!

Band leader Len Joy was about to be beamed coast to coast for a new Coca-Cola radio program. On the way, the crew realized there was no theme song. So, Joy plunked out 32 bars that evening. And the title? At the top of the work paper he jotted a note to himself — "Coca-Cola Signature" — and they used this as the title! Joy set the tempo to a tango beat, but when no one liked it he threw out the brass and slowed it to a graceful waltz. It was a hit! But few people ever really remember the tune; it was the band's lead-in song, and usually faded away. Those of you who can peck out a song on the piano might want to just play the first five bars above - you will remember what is being forgotten! On April 22, 1932, Len Joy assigned all rights to the theme song to the Coca-Cola Company.

1950s, Eddie Fisher for Coca-Cola, "My Friend." $20.

1970s, Superman record with sleeve. $40.

1920, music and words for "Oh! Mother." $40.

1920, "Oh! Mother I'm Wild." $40.

1970s, W.C. Fields, record with sleeve. $40.

1970s, Dick Tracy, 78 RPM with sleeve. $40.

1970s, "All Summer Long,: 12 hits on a 78 RPM record. $40.

1944, the Andrews Sisters, "Rum and Coca-Cola." $25.

1944, the Andrews Sisters, "Rum and Coca-Cola." $25.

1970s, Sgt. Preston record with sleeve. $40.

1970s, Lone Ranger record with sleeve. $40.

1940s & '50s, "March King" concert band organ: 232 pipes, 16 rank, transported on a 1941 Chevy Coke delivery truck. Courtesy of Coca-Cola Bottling Co., Kokomo, IN. PRICELESS.

1950s, Eddie Fisher, 78 RPM with sleeve. $35.

1930s, Ray Noble, "Refreshment Time," round cardboard, 2-1/2" glass bottle. $225.

1960s, 45 RPM "Swing the Jingle" with sleeve. $25.

45 RPM - Swingers For Coke, 1970s. $20.

1950s, Eddie Fisher, 45 RPM "Rum & Coca-Cola" from MCA. $30.

1960s, Artist Record, 78 RPM. $40.

1960s, Gene Rayburn, 33-1/3 RPM. $30.

1950s, Tony Bennett, 45 RPM with sleeve. $25.

1971, 45 RPM "It's The Real Thing." $15.

1960s, Trini Lopez, 45 RPM with sleeve. $20.

1969, "It's The Real Thing." $10.

"Trip To The Moon" record and sleeve. $75.

1970s, Fortunes, 78 RPM. $35.

1971, Seekers, 45 RPM "Teach The World." $25.

Jam Handy, 33-1/3 RPM. $40.

1960s, The Shirelles, 45 RPM with sleeve. $35.

1960s, "ZING! with Coca-Cola" poster. $35.

1974, "Look Up America." $10.

"The Great Get Together," San Francisco. $50.

1971, "I'd Like to Buy the World a Coke. $10.

1972, "Country Sunshine." $10.

1970s, Coca-Cola harmonica. $85.

1950s, leatherette carrier for records. $65.

1940s, The Andrews Sisters, "Rum and Coca-Cola." $30.

1960s, training record, 33-1/3 RPM. $35.

MISCELLANEOUS

1960s, circus program back cover.

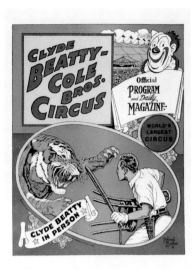

1960s, Clyde Beatty circus program, front. $25.

1960s, bronze, bottle-shaped book ends. $250 pr.

1920s, metal bell. $550.

1920s, metal sandwich toaster, 7-5/8" diameter. $1000.

1936, aluminum pretzel bowl. $375.

1940s, metal dish embossed with hand holding bottle, 4" diameter. $175.

LILLIAN NORDICA

This is a poster of Lillian Nordica - star of the Metropolitan Opera Company. It is the largest (26" x 46") of three 1905 posters for which she posed. To find a cardboard poster of this size in such excellent condition is RARE. It is valued at $13,000.

WHISTLES

1920s, cardboard, 3-3/4", rare. $425.

1920s, yellow, wooden. $150.

1920s, yellow & red, tin. $150.

1920s & '30s, aluminum whistling thimble. $85.

1920s, yellow, tin. $200.

1950s, white plastic. $40.

1970s, bottom of the plastic boat whistle. $30.

1970s, boat-shaped plastic whistle.

1970s, Mexican bottle cap whistle. $5.

MATCHBOOKS

FRONT

BACK

1914. $575.

1930s. $175.

number:date:		value:	
1	unknown	$275	
2	1960	$40	
3	1930	$25	
4	1920	$30	
5	1930	$25	
6	1936	$25	50th anniv.
7	1960s	$30	
8	1950s	$15	
9	1950s	$15	
10	1950s	$15	
11	1960s	$15	
12	1960s	$15	
13	1960s	$30	
14	1950s	$15	
15	1960s	$15	worlds fair
16	1960s	$15	
17	1970s	$10	

LAYOUT SHEETS FOR ADVERTISING

1970s. $8.

1970s. $8.

1960s. $3.

1970s. $8.

1960s. $5.

1950s. $3.

1950s. $3.

1960s. $5.

1950s. $5.

1950s. $8.

1950s. $8.

1960s. $5.

1950s. $3.

1950s. $5.

1950s. $5.

1960s. $5.

1950s. $3.

1960s. $5.

1960. $5.

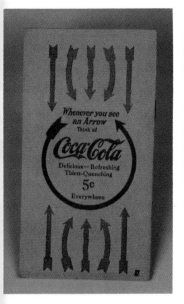

1912, "The Truth About Coca-Cola," 16 pages. $40.

1930s & '40s, annual reports to stockholders. $35 ea.

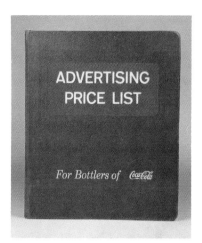

1950s, "Advertising Price List" for bottlers of Coca-Cola. $300.

1950s & '60s, catalog of merchandising equipment for Coca-Cola. $350 ea.

1950s, Vendo cooler equipment. $35.

$2, $5, and $10 coin wrappers. $10 ea.

1920s, shipping case address tag, Bogalusa, LA. $8.

Advertisements. $10.

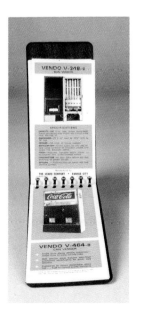

1940s, Vendo sales book of coolers. $35.

1959, advertisement for a bottlers' convention. $15.

"More Profit To You" brochure. $10.

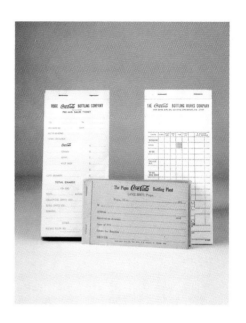

Salesmen's and drivers' route books. $10 ea.

Westinghouse coolers for Coca-Cola. $35.

1930s & '40s, driver's license holder. $10.

Advertisement. $10.

1941, list of hospitals selling Coca-Cola. $40.

1970s, leverage packaging strategy. $25.

Tag from a piece of Coca-Cola clothing. $5.

"Your Best Customers" brochure. $10.

MISCELLANEOUS

Wood frames litho inserts, top, 62-3/8" x 33-1/4", $300; bottom, 20" x 36". $300.

1977, invitation to reception, Huntsville, Ala. 1977 Coca-Cola National Convention. $35.

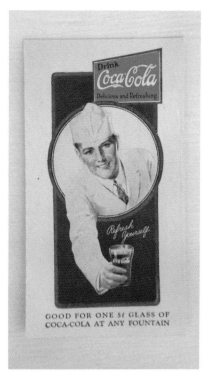

1920, soda jerk illustrated coupon, 2-1/4" x 4". $40.

1960s, two-sided cardboard snowman bottle display or dangler, 17-1/4" x 9-3/4". $100.

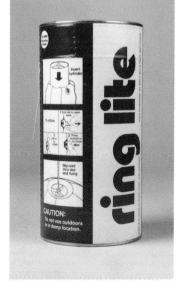

1970s, inflatable ring light, M.I.B. $45.

1960, a single-sided sailboat display for king-sized bottles, 22-1/2" x 14". $75.

1960's, "Case of Bottles" fan, plant tour gift. $20.

1950s, plant tour gift, "Fan Flare Coca-Cola." $20.

1970s, pulsating black light. $40.

251

1927

1930

1934-35

1931

1928

1951

1928

Index

New Application For Membership

APPLICATION FOR MEMBERSHIP AND RENEWAL

☐ Renewal   Account # _____   ☐ New   ☐ Address Change

(check one and include account # if renewing)

Primary: **Associates:**
$ 30 US $ 35 Canada $ 50 Overseas–Airmail $ 5 each

Name : _____

Address: _____

City: _____ State:___Zip: _____Country_____

Phone _____E-mail: _____

Associates:_____
_____

Do You Belong to a Chapter?____Yes____No If yes, list main affiliation_____

Total annual membership $ _____

Number of years (cannot exceed 3) 1 ☐   2 ☐   3 ☐   X _____

Total amount enclosed (in US funds, payable through US or Canadian bank) $ _____

Visa or MasterCard#_____Exp Date_____Signature_____

___I do not want my address in a directory   ___I do not want my address given to any third party

Credit Card Payments can be faxed to: 404-728-9882
Make check or money order payable in US funds to: **CCCC**
Mail to: **The Coca-Cola Collectors Club**
Membership, P.O. Box 49166, Atlanta, GA 30359-1166

DIR. 99

Not sponsored by The Coca-Cola Company. Trademarks used with permission

1950s, window display.